AF450230

BOOK COLLECTING

LECTOR HOUSE PUBLIC DOMAIN WORKS

This book is a result of an effort made by Lector House towards making a contribution to the preservation and repair of original classic literature. The original text is in the public domain in the United States of America, and possibly other countries depending upon their specific copyright laws.

In an attempt to preserve, improve and recreate the original content, certain conventional norms with regard to typographical mistakes, hyphenations, punctuations and/or other related subject matters, have been corrected upon our consideration. However, few such imperfections might not have been rectified as they were inherited and preserved from the original content to maintain the authenticity and construct, relevant to the work. The work might contain a few prior copyright references as well as page references which have been retained, wherever considered relevant to the part of the construct. We believe that this work holds historical, cultural and/or intellectual importance in the literary works community, therefore despite the oddities, we accounted the work for print as a part of our continuing effort towards preservation of literary work and our contribution towards the development of the society as a whole, driven by our beliefs.

We are grateful to our readers for putting their faith in us and accepting our imperfections with regard to preservation of the historical content. We shall strive hard to meet up to the expectations to improve further to provide an enriching reading experience.

Though, we conduct extensive research in ascertaining the status of copyright before redeveloping a version of the content, in rare cases, a classic work might be incorrectly marked as not-in-copyright. In such cases, if you are the copyright holder, then kindly contact us or write to us, and we shall get back to you with an immediate course of action.

HAPPY READING!

BOOK COLLECTING

JOHN HERBERT SLATER

ISBN: 978-93-5420-769-3

Published: 1892

© 2021
LECTOR HOUSE LLP

LECTOR HOUSE LLP
E-MAIL: lectorpublishing@gmail.com

AN OLD PRINTING PRESS.

From the Quintilian of Vascosan, folio, Paris, 1538.

BOOK COLLECTING
A GUIDE FOR AMATEURS

BY

J. H. SLATER

Editor of *Book Prices Current;* formerly Editor of *Book Lore;*
Author of *The Library Manual; Engravings and their Value;*
The Law relating to Copyright and Trade Marks, etc., etc.

1892

CONTENTS

CHAPTER I.

THE Bibliophile, as he is somewhat pedantically termed, probably dates his existence from the time when books began to be multiplied in sufficient quantities to render the acquisition of duplicate copies by the public a matter of possibility, but his opportunities of amassing a large number of volumes can hardly be said to have arisen until many years after the invention of printing.

The most ancient manuscript extant has been identified with the reign of Amenophis, who ruled in Egypt no less than 1600 years before the Christian era, and this manuscript, old as it is, shows such superior execution that there can be little, if any, doubt that caligraphy in its oldest—that is, its hieroglyphic—form must be referred for its origin to a period still more remote. Diodorus Siculus relates that Rameses II. founded a library in one of the chambers of the Memnonium at Thebes, and deposited therein the 42 sacred books of Thoth, which had they been in existence now would be nearly 5000 years old. In those days, however, education was looked upon as the peculiar property of the priesthood; the library had sealed doors; even the very books themselves must have been wholly unintelligible to all but the favoured few whose duty it was to preserve them with religious care. All the early Egyptian manuscripts extant have served in their day an ecclesiastical rather than a secular object, and all of them abound with mythological stories more or less recondite. To use the art of writing for any less sacred purpose would have been held disrespectful to the educated class and resented accordingly. Ptolemy Sotor, who reigned over Egypt about the year 280 B.C., appears to have been the first to break through the artificial barrier which the priestcraft of age upon age had succeeded in building up; and his magnificent twin library at Alexandria, known as the Bruchium and Serapeum, which was partly stocked with the confiscated books of travellers who touched at the port, became in course of time the most famous in the world, and would most probably have been so at this day had it not been destroyed by Theodosius and his army, as a sacrifice at the shrine of ignorance and superstition. With the destruction of the library at Alexandria, containing, as it did, books which can never be replaced, the literary importance of the Egyptians came to an end; thenceforward all that remained was the consciousness of having instructed others better able to preserve their independence than they were themselves. Yet after all it is somewhat extraordinary that Egypt should have been not merely the first to encourage a love of literature, but also the last; for simultaneously with the destruction of the Bruchium and Serapeum were ushered in the first centuries of the dark ages, when the ability to read and write was looked upon as unworthy the status of a free man, unless indeed he were a priest, and when fire and sword were brought into requisition for the purpose of annihilating everything that suggested mental culture.

In the eras which intervened between the reign of Rameses the Constructor and that of Theodosius the Destroyer, Pisistratus had founded his public library at Athens, and collected the poems of Homer which had previously been scattered in detached portions throughout Greece; and Plato, the prince of ancient book hunters, had given no less than 100 attic minæ—nearly £300 of our money—for three small treatises of Philolaus the Pythagorean. Aristotle too, unless he has been sadly maligned, thought 300 minæ a fair exchange for a little pile of books which had formerly belonged to Speusippus, thereby setting an example to that French king of after ages who pawned his gold and silver plate to obtain means wherewith to purchase a coveted copy of Lacertius, as Gabriel Naudé calls the great Epicurean biographer. In Rome also Lucullus had furnished his house with books and thrown open his doors to all who wished to consult them. Atticus the famous publisher had turned out a thousand copies of the second book of Martial's *Epigrams*, with its 540 lines of verse, bound and endorsed in the space of a single hour, and the booksellers carried on a flourishing trade in their shops in the Argeletum and the Vicus Sandalarius, exhibiting catalogues on the side posts of their doors exactly as the second-hand dealers in London and elsewhere do now. Of all this vast enterprise of Greece and Rome not a trace remains: only the sepulchral writings of mother Egypt and the clay tablets of Assyria.

History tells us how the luxurious rich of Athens and Rome regarded their books as so many pieces of furniture, and engaged learned slaves to read aloud at their banquets; and if the example of Plato were followed to any extent, doubtless large sums of money were spent on rare originals which had passed through the hands of a succession of dilettanti, and acquired thereby a reputation for genuineness, which they could not have gained in any other manner. Seneca indeed ridicules the vulgar emulation which prompted some of his contemporaries to collect volumes of which, he says, they knew nothing except the outsides, many of them possibly barely that. It has been ever so: in England to-day there are many who would have felt the lash of Nero's tutor across their shoulders.

When the public no longer took pleasure in mental culture, and the whole world was overrun with hordes of barbarians intent upon destruction, learning of every kind was banished to the monasteries, and the monks became the only book lovers, making it their business to transcribe, generation after generation, the volumes which had been saved from the general conflagration. It is entirely through their efforts that the old classics have been preserved to our day; we have to thank them, and them alone, for the preservation of the Bible itself. Even in the monasteries, however, the same spirit of emulation which had prompted Greek to compete with Greek, and Roman with Roman, became apparent in course of time. Ordinary transcripts, though never numerous, began to be looked upon as hardly pretentious enough, and the larger houses established *scriptoria*, where trained monks sat the livelong day, painfully tracing letter after letter on the purest vellum, while Bibliolatrists added illuminated borders and miniatures in a style that would task the skill of our best artists of to-day. This competition led to the exchange of manuscripts, or to their loan for a brief period, so that by degrees monastic libraries assumed large proportions, numbering many hundreds of neatly bound volumes, which, on being opened, looked as though printed, so accurately and carefully had the copying been done. This explains how Fust, the inventor, or one of the inventors, of printing, was enabled to deceive the people of Paris, for he flooded the market there with printed copies of the Bible which he sold for 50 crowns each, instead of for 400 or 500 crowns, which would have been a fair price had they been in manuscript. The book buyers of Paris *thought they were in manuscript*, until the recurrence of one or two defective types cast from the same matrix caused an inquiry. Fust was arrested, not for the fraud but for witchcraft, and to save his life he explained his process. Thus did the old order give place to the new.

In a very few years after the discovery of Fust's secret the whole of the western portion of Europe was dotted with printing presses. Before 1499 there were 236 in operation; and six years after Gutenberg had completed his Bible of 42 lines there were no less than 50 German cities and towns in which presses had been established. Considering that this only brings us down to about the year 1462, it is evident with what rapidity the art of printing was seized upon through the length and breadth of the country of its probable origin.

In 1475 our own famous printer Caxton was being instructed in the office of Colard Mansion at Bruges, and in 1477, if not earlier,[1] he settled as a printer at Westminster, thus laying the foundation of our English industry and establishing a native press which has continued to grow year by year until it has assumed its present enormous proportions. Authorities, however, point out that improvement in the art of printing did not come by age or experience, for, curiously enough, the science—for such it really is—was almost perfect from its origin, and, so far as this country is concerned, has distinctly deteriorated since the death of Caxton and his pupils Wynkyn de Worde, Faques, and Pynson. The typefounders of that early period were as expert as many at the present day and immeasurably superior to most. The greatest care appears to have been exercised in the casting, and competition did not engender the slovenly haste which is only too apparent in many of our modern publications. It is probable that, simultaneously with the introduction of printing into England, a certain limited few, most likely ecclesiastics and powerful nobles, would commence to collect works from the press of Caxton, and subsequently from the foreign presses. In 1545 the Earl of Warwick's library consisted of 40 printed books, in 1691 that of the Rev. Richard Baxter of 1448. It is not until a comparatively modern period that any single man has been able to mass together thousands of volumes during the course of a single lifetime, for it

[1] *The Dictes and Sayinges of the Philosophers,* Caxton's first book which bears a date, was finished in November, 1477; and it is upon the strength of this that the Caxton Quarcentenary Festival was held in 1877. There can be little doubt, however, that he printed many books of which no copies remain, some of which were probably earlier than *The Dictes.*

is only recently that printing has been used on every trivial occasion, and in the manufacture of books which would originally have been deemed unworthy of the application of the art.

At the present day books constitute one of the necessities of life and private libraries one of its luxuries. The collector has such ample scope for the exercise of his favourite pursuit that it has long since become a question not so much of accumulating a large number of miscellaneous volumes, as of exercising a rigid discrimination and confining one's attention to works of a certain class, to the almost entire exclusion of all others. Thus, some book hunters collect first, or, at any rate, early, editions of popular modern authors, such, for example, as Dickens, Thackeray, and Lever; others collect old editions of the Scriptures, a few, the expensive early printed volumes which are every year becoming absorbed into the public libraries, and consequently growing more scarce. A small number attempt to form an extensive all-round library, but they rarely, if ever, succeed, partly because life is too short for the purpose, and money too limited in quantity. Occasionally a large collection comes to the auctioneer's hammer, but in nearly every instance it will be found that it represents the labours of several generations of owners, each of whom has contributed the principal publications of his day or taken advantage of any proffered bargain which he may have happened to come across during the course of his lifetime.

The book lover however is not content with mere acquisition, he feels it his duty to know something of the inner life, so to speak, of each volume on his shelf—something, that is to say, beyond the outside lettering. He wishes to know the chief incidents in the history of the person who wrote it, under what circumstances it was written and why, how many editions have been published, whether the particular copy is perfect, how much it is worth from a pecuniary point of view, and occasionally the nature of the contents. The word "occasionally" may be considered by some as used in an objectionable sense, implying in fact that book lovers are not always in the habit of reading what they possess. Let the collector of Bibles say whether he is in the habit of reading the various editions which he has been at such pains to collect, and it will then be time enough to inquire into the practices of other collectors who, like himself, though in different departments, may not consider themselves justified in spending the amount of time necessary for careful and satisfactory study. In truth, if all books were read, it is only reasonable to suppose that all libraries would be small; and, as we know the contrary to be the fact, we must acknowledge the truth of the main proposition to a very large extent. The happiness of the book lover, as we know him when in the plenitude of his glory, consists by no means in reading, but in the contemplation of his possessions from afar; an inane treatise on theology becomes the object of his daily prayers when bound in morocco and stamped with the Golden Fleece of Longepierre.

In this short dissertation we have but little to do with the contents of any book. This knowledge can be acquired as circumstances and opportunity offer; we deal rather with extraneous details which are necessary to be known by everyone who aspires to form a collection of books for himself and would know something of the history of each.

Every bibliographer, and also every collector of any eminence, has within reach certain books of reference which experience has shown to be absolutely necessary. Chief among these is Lowndes' *Bibliographer's Manual* of which two editions have been issued. The first was published in 1834; the second in seven parts from 1857-61, with an appendix volume in 1864, having been re-issued from the stereotype plates without a date in 1871. The latter may frequently be picked up at auction sales for about 25s., but there is this peculiarity about the work, that it really would not seem to be very material which edition is purchased. The book is imperfect and full of errors: it cannot be relied on, and the second edition, which was edited by the late Mr. H. G. Bohn, the eminent bookseller, is as untrustworthy as the first edition. The original plan, which has never been departed from, was to give the names of English authors in alphabetical order, placing under each the title of the works he wrote, with the date of each edition, number of volumes, in many cases the collation, and finally the sums realised at auction. Nothing fluctuates so greatly as auction values, and it is not surprising, therefore, to find that not a single entry in Lowndes under this head can be accepted at the present day. Some of the variations between past and present prices are ludicrous in the extreme, and there is no doubt that anyone who attempted to obtain his knowledge of the value of books from Lowndes' *Manual* would find himself in possession of a mass of old-time information which would be rather a hindrance to him than otherwise. The *Manual* is useful because it gives a full and tolerably complete list of English authors, and collates many of their works with considerable care; it is, moreover, the authority quoted by cataloguers, and, being a copyright publication, practically bars the way to any rival work on the same subject. For these and other reasons it is indispensable.

To ascertain the value of a book is an exceedingly difficult operation; in fact, there are many who assert that it is impossible to do so. Booksellers' prices, as disclosed in their catalogues, are not much to go by, for it is notorious that a West End dealer will often charge more than one who is established further East. Again, some London booksellers charge more or less than provincial ones, according to circumstance and the character of their customers. Until recently there were only two ways of becoming an adept in this department, the first and best by practical experience, a method which is not, of course, available to any but dealers and their assistants; and the second, by indexing retail catalogues and striking an average. A third method, that of taking the average of auction sales, was not available until recently, for it is too troublesome, for any save those whose business it is, to attend sales by auction all day long for nine months out of the twelve, in order to obtain the necessary materials.

In 1886, I conceived the idea of fully reporting all sales of any importance taking place either in London or the provinces, and in December of that year the necessary arrangements were completed, with the modification that for the present, at any rate, no notice was to be taken of any book which did not realise at least 20s. by auction. This publication, the success of which amply demonstrates the necessity for its existence, is named *Book Prices Current*, and already five volumes are published, and a sixth will be ready at the beginning of next year (1893). As a book of this kind would be useless without a full index, the greatest possible care has been taken to make it as complete and as accurate as possible. From *Book Prices Current* a very good idea of the average value of almost any book may be obtained. Careful note of the way in which the particular volume is bound must, of course, be taken, for this, as might be expected, makes a great difference in the price.

The French are supposed to be much better bibliographers than our own countrymen, and if the character of the authoritative works published in either country is a criterion of national merit there cannot be much, if any, doubt that this is so. Lowndes' *Bibliographer's Manual* takes no notice of books published abroad, and, as they are in the majority, it becomes necessary to seek an additional guide. This is afforded by Brunet's *Manuel du Libraire et de l'Amateur de Livres*, published at Paris in 6 vols. from 1860-65, and usually found, with the Appendix on *Géographie*, 1870, and 2 vol. *Supplément*, 1878-80. In its place it is a much better book than Lowndes', but it is very expensive, frequently bringing as much as £10 and £12 by auction. Here again, however, the values are quite unreliable, and, as in the case of Lowndes', there is no index of subjects whatever. From the three works mentioned very much may undoubtedly be learned about almost any book provided the author's name be known; but as it frequently happened that many authors chose, for reasons satisfactory to themselves, to conceal their names altogether, or in the much commoner instance of the name being forgotten by or unknown to the searcher, an index of subjects becomes a necessity. This is partly supplied by Watt's *Bibliotheca Britannica* in 4 vols. 4to, 1824, two volumes being devoted to authors and two to subjects, there being also cross references from one to the other. This inestimable work occupied the author the greater portion of his life, and is a monument of industry and research. The auction value amounts to £3 within a fraction, this being one of the few books which has a fixed market price all over the kingdom. Good copies in handsome bindings frequently occur, and are worth £4 to £5. The *English Catalogue*, initiated by the late Mr. Sampson Low, is a periodical which makes its appearance annually, and, unlike all the other works I have mentioned, is confined entirely to current literature. The title of every work published during the year is given, with the month in which it was issued, the price, and publisher's name, the whole being arranged in one line under the name of the author. At intervals, which do not appear to be strictly defined, collective editions of these annual catalogues, arranged in one alphabet, are published, as well as of the indexes of the *titles* which are appended to each annual issue.[2]

It is obvious that a work of this kind must be of the greatest utility, and as the *English Catalogue* is merely a continuation of the *London Catalogue* and the *British Catalogue*, the former of which commenced so far back as the year 1811, it will be seen that a comprehensive view can be taken of the whole range of English literature from that date to the present. The *Catalogue* has not, however, always been so carefully prepared as it is now, and consequently in the earlier days many publications were omitted. When this is the case Lowndes and Watt will be found of material assistance, the latter especially. A complete set of these catalogues, unfortunately, is very difficult to obtain, and as the earlier ones are not indispensable, it

[2] In the annual volume for 1891 a new scheme has been started, the authors and titles entries appearing in *one* alphabet in "dictionary form".

may be perhaps advisable to forego them and to commence in 1814. The volumes to be acquired therefore would be *London Catalogue*, 1816-51; *English Catalogue*, 1835-63, 1863-71, 1872-80, 1881-89; with the accompanying subject indexes to the *London Catalogue*, 1814-46; and to the *English Catalogue*, 1835-55, 1856-75, 1874 (*sic*)-80. It will be noticed that the dates sometimes overlap each over, but this is an advantage rather than a drawback. Among the other books frequently consulted by both dealers and amateurs are Mr. Swan Sonnenschein's *The Best Books*; the *Reference Catalogue of Current Literature*, and Halkett & Laing's *Dictionary of Anonymous and Pseudonymous Literature of Great Britain*, in 4 vols. These are mentioned together because they are essentially subject indexes and the best of their kind.

Sonnenschein's *The Best Books*, already in a second and vastly improved edition, is a comparatively recent publication, in which, under subjects arranged systematically, are placed the best current books, whether ancient or modern, on each subject, with the prices, sizes, publisher's name and dates of the first and last editions of each. There are about 50,000 works included, and they together give a very good idea of all the material in the various departments of research which the specialist is likely to have occasion to read or refer to. Old books are included where they are of actual present-day value to the student. The selection is not, of course, entirely made by the author, as it is impossible for him to have read a hundredth part of the books recommended; most probably the list has been compiled from the works of specialists, the various encyclopædias, and so forth; but however this may be, it is a very useful one in the hands of a person capable of discrimination (towards which the numerous critical and bibliographical notes and the system of asterisks are a great help), especially if he live near one or other of the large libraries now springing up in different parts of the country.

The *Reference Catalogue of Current Literature*, a cumbrous and unwieldy tome, the last issue of which was out of print within a couple of months of its publication, consists of a large number of publishers' catalogues arranged in alphabetical order. Each work mentioned is indexed, and this has been accomplished so fully and accurately that almost any book to be bought new in the market makes its appearance here.

Halkett & Laing's *Dictionary* is, as the title implies, a record of the anonymous and pseudonymous literature of Great Britain. If an author wrote under an assumed name or anonymously, his real name will be found here, together with a short account of his publications. This work can hardly be said to be indispensable, but it is, notwithstanding, exceedingly useful, and well worth the three and a half guineas which will have to be expended upon it.

Among other works which at one time were thought more of than they are now is Quaritch's *Catalogue of Books*, in one thick volume, 1880, and a supplement which is back-dated 1875-7. The chief value of this lay not only in the prices, which were, as in every other bookseller's catalogue, appended to the items, but in the extraordinary number of the entries, which cover the whole range of British and foreign literature. Even now the work is useful, but there is no doubt that it is gradually decreasing in importance, owing to the high-class works of reference which have lately made their appearance. As to values, *Book Prices Current* gives them much more satisfactorily than any bookseller can pretend or afford to do, while most of the bibliographical notes and references are to be found in one or other of the works I have mentioned.

The collector who, as yet, is not sufficiently advanced to fully realise the difficulties he will have to surmount before he can bring together a judicious assortment of books, will at any rate begin to see that the knowledge requisite to enable him to do so is of no mean order. The preliminaries will take him a long time to master, and he will find that the expense is a factor by no means to be despised. Even the books mentioned are not all that he may have to procure, for if, after consideration, he should decide to devote his attention exclusively to one branch of Bibliography, there are other books of reference to be purchased, and a special course of study must be entered upon and carefully followed, if he would hope to be successful. Thus, should he decide to make Dickens or Thackeray his one author, as so many people are doing now, he will need a guide to direct his course. Memory is so treacherous that he can take nothing on trust, and time so short that he cannot afford to journey two sides of the triangle when he might have taken the third. These special works for special departments are set out and enlarged upon in the following chapter, but before referring to them it may not be superfluous to remind the reader that a book of reference only possesses a relative value. It is quite possible to have a whole library within reach and yet to be ignorant of the proper method of using it. Some of our best writers had no library worthy the name, but the few books they had they knew — knew, that is to say, how to extract the information they required, which book to consult, how it was arranged, and what might be expected of it. Though a book collector is not necessarily a book reader, he will have to be absolute master of his works of reference, or he will find every volume on his shelf a useless incumbrance. Where to possess all the absolute facts is of importance, the newest works are, generally speaking, most likely to be the best; but this is very far from being applicable to a library in all its departments. Yet even in the case of works of a general nature a careful and economic selection may be made, so as to cover, in a small compass, much valuable ground.

CHAPTER II.

THE FIRST ENGLISH AUCTION SALE—FASHION IN BOOK COL-
LECTING—SPECIAL BOOKS OF REFERENCE RELATING TO
PARTICULAR BRANCHES OF BIBLIOGRAPHY.

T HE first sale of books by auction which is recorded as having taken place
in England was held in Warwick Lane exactly 213 years ago, and Dr. Lazarus Seaman, whose library was dispersed on the occasion in question, appears to have
confined his attention strictly to Latin Bibles of the 16th century, the cumbrous
works of the Puritan divines, and the great editions of the Fathers—huge folios
thought so little of that, allowing for the change in the value of money, they can
now for the most part be bought from the booksellers for less than they could then
at auction. The reason which prompted this old collector to limit his purchases to
works of a single class was in all probability much the same as that which prevails
under similar circumstances at the present time, namely, a natural desire for finali-
ty, the outcome of an experience which shows plainly enough that in order to form
a complete collection of anything its scope must be reduced to the smallest possible
compass. As a matter of fact Dr. Seaman appears to have embarked on a somewhat
extensive undertaking, for in the period mentioned by far the greater majority of
works issued from the press were of a religious nature. Still the incident is valuable from an antiquarian point of view, as it forms a good precedent for a large
body of modern collectors who, like Seaman, follow the prevailing fashion of the
day. This fashion on being analysed will be found to vary at different periods and
to be of longer or shorter duration according to a variety of circumstances which
appear to be entirely without the range of argumentative discussion.

In the year 1699, for example, a book was published, entitled *Entretiens sur
les Contes de Fées*, in which one of the characters is described as saying, "For some
time past you know to what an extent the editions of the Elzevirs have been in demand. The fancy for them has penetrated far and wide to such an extent, indeed,
that I know a man who starves himself for the sake of accumulating as many of
these books as he can lay his hands on." In the chapter devoted to the Elzevir
press, these important publications are treated as fully as space permits, so that
at present it will be sufficient to say that for nearly 200 years many generations of
collectors have made painstaking attempts to form a complete library of these little
books, which, after all, excel only in the quality of the paper and the beauty of the
type. For real scholarly merit the editions of Gryphius or Estienne are much to be
preferred, but this makes no difference. The Elzevirs were fashionable, much more
so than they are now, and accordingly they were valued. It is, moreover, quite pos-

sible that they may again rise in popular favour, in which event those far-seeing individuals who are even now imitating the example of the collector mentioned in the *Entretiens* will reap a rich harvest in case they choose to avail themselves of it. The great guide-book on the productions of this famous press is that by Alphonse Willems, entitled *Les Elzevier, Histoire et Annales Typographiques*, published at Brussels in 1880, with the *Etudes sur la Bibliographie Elzevirienne* of Dr. G. Berghman, a kind of supplement to it, published at Stockholm in 1885.[3]

Each publication is given in the order in which it was issued, and what will be found especially useful is an appendix containing a list of the spurious Elzevirs issued from the Dutch presses and of the forgeries which have from time to time been foisted on the confiding amateur. With the assistance of this work, the Elzevir collector cannot go very far wrong, though he will undoubtedly have much to learn from his own practical experience. He will become more or less perfect in his lesson in time, and may take comfort in the reflection that nothing so quickly ensures perfection as a limited series of bad mistakes. As examples of the Elzevir press are of "right" and "wrong" editions, with and without red lines, and are, moreover, usually measured in millimetres with the assistance of a rule which the enthusiastic collector invariably carries about with him wherever he goes, it is evident that there is much to learn and a great deal to be carried in the memory before the amateur can trust himself to become his own mentor.

Difficult as the subject of the Elzevir press is, that of the Aldine press is more so. It was established much earlier—*viz.*, about 1489—and examples are more numerous and altogether more confusing. As a general rule they are also more expensive, and none but rich collectors can afford to compete for examples of the best class. Still, good specimens may occasionally be got for reasonable sums; and as a guide to the subject as a whole Renouard's *Annales de l'Imprimerie des Alde* (1st ed., 2 vols., Paris, 1803; 2nd, 3 vols., *ib.*, 1825; 3rd, 1 vol., *ib.*, 1834) occupies a unique position. This work is arranged on a similar plan to the *Elzevier* and is quite as indispensable to the specialist. An ordinary copy of the 2nd ed. will cost about 30s., but the more recent edition can sometimes be got for considerably less.

Those fortunate persons who succeed in forming a good library of early printed books usually consult Dibdin's *Bibliotheca Spenceriana*, which professes to be nothing more than a descriptive catalogue of books of the 15th century in the incomparable collection of Earl Spencer. It is, however, full of notes by one of the best of English bibliographers. The British Museum *Catalogue of Early Printed Books in English*, 3 vols., 1884, which is carried down to 1640, and Maitland's *Early Printed Books in Lambeth Library*, 1843, carried down to 1600, are also frequently consulted. These works are of course supplementary to Lowndes' *Bibliographer's Manual* and Watt's *Bibliotheca Britannica*, which, as previously explained, are on the shelves of every collector worthy the name, be he a specialist or not. The department of early printed books may, however, be left without further comment, as not one

[3] To those who do not read French or do not possess *Les Elzevier*, Mr. Goldsmid's *The Elzevir Presses*, published as part of his *Bibliotheca Curiosa*, may be of some assistance. It is a species of compendium of the work of M. Willems, and was issued in 1889. It is somewhat faulty and incomplete; but not without its value to beginners in the study of the Elzevir press.

person out of many thousands is able for obvious reasons to devote his serious attention to it. Public libraries and similar institutions, which may be said to have a continuing existence, frequently contain a good show of works of this class, and, in the opinion of many, are the only suitable repositories for them.

Privately printed books are those which are issued either from a private press or for the benefit of private friends. They are never published in the ordinary acceptation of that term, and cannot be bought at first hand. A good collection of these is of course difficult, though by no means impossible, to acquire; and for the benefit of those who may wish to devote themselves to this department—uninteresting as it undoubtedly is—Martin's *Privately Printed Books* (1834, 2nd ed., 1854), in 1 vol. 8vo, is readily available. Many of these so-called "books" consist merely of single sheets of letterpress; others, on the contrary, are more pretentious. In the former case they are more correctly termed "broadsides"; and R. Lemon's *Catalogue of the Collection of Broadsides, in the possession of the Society of Antiquaries* (8vo, 1866), though by no means a perfect book, is certainly the best that can be procured for our purpose.

Early printed American books, or those which in any way relate to the American Continent, provided only they were published during the 16th or 17th centuries, have lately become exceedingly scarce. In June, 1888, nine small quarto tracts, bound in one volume, brought, £66 by auction, a record entirely surpassed by the preceding lot, which, consisting of twelve similar tracts only, brought no less a sum than £555. These prices are of course highly exceptional; but so great is the desire to obtain books of this class that the amounts in question, exorbitant though they may appear to be, were perhaps not excessive.

The amateur may in this instance follow the rule with every confidence. Should he at any time see a work relating to America, no matter where printed so long as it is dated before the year 1700, he should on no account pass it by without very careful consideration; and the same remark applies, though to a less extent, to all books printed in Scotland before that date. In both cases it is probable that the specimen offered for sale will have a most unprepossessing exterior, and in some instances the price asked may be small. This frequently happens, since the more uneducated class of dealers commence by valuing a book from its appearance, and while a coloured plate or two would at once put them on the *qui vive* there is generally nothing about books of this kind which *looks* valuable. It is no disparagement to the trade as a whole to say that some booksellers, particularly those who carry on business in small provincial towns, are absolutely ignorant of anything more than the first principles of their trade, and it is out of these that bargains are made. Henry Stevens' *Catalogue of the American Books in the Library of the British Museum* (1886, 8vo) is from the pen of a late famous bookseller who made many "bargains" in his time and whose profound knowledge of the insides as well as of the outsides of his very valuable collection was in every way worthy of his success.

Shakespearian collectors cannot do better than consult the article "Shakespeare" in Lowndes' *Bibliographer's Manual*, where every known edition, translation, and commentary professes to be catalogued and also in many cases collated and described. Some of Halliwell-Phillipps' works, though not absolutely indispensable, are nevertheless exceedingly useful.

Bible collectors do not as a rule notice editions later than what is styled the "Vinegar" Bible, published in 1717. They commence with Coverdale's issue of 1535, and proceed onward in regular order, for the most part arranging their collection not according to date but under the various "versions". This subject is very extensive and exceedingly difficult to handle, so much so that, without a competent guide, it will be found impossible to make satisfactory progress. This is provided in Cotton's *Editions of the Bible and Parts thereof in English* (1821, 2nd ed., 1852), and J. R. Dore's *Old Bibles* (1876, 2nd ed., 1888). Mr. Dore is probably the best living authority upon English Bibles and Testaments, and his book is in itself amply sufficient for the amateur. It is published by Eyre & Spottiswoode at 5s.

For works on botany consult Pritzel's *Thesaurus Literaturæ Botanicæ* (Leipsic, 1847-51, 2nd ed., 1872-7, 4to); and for books exclusively relating to tobacco, some of which are very rare and valuable, W. Bragge's *Bibliotheca Nicotiana* (priv. prin., r. 8vo, 1880).

Angling and the whole of the literature devoted to it is dealt with in Westwood's new *Bibliotheca Piscatoria* (1883), and swimming in R. Thomas' *Bibliographical List of Works on Swimming* (1868, 8vo).

The Greek and Latin Classics were at one time great favourites with all classes of collectors, but of late they have fallen considerably from their high estate. Many of the early editions, being printed by famous houses, as the *editio princeps* of Virgil's works was, which sold for £590 at the Hopetoun House dispersion, a few months ago, are still eagerly sought after, but not *quâ* classics—merely as specimens of ancient typography. Ordinary editions of Horace, Virgil, Sallust, Plato, Livy, and the rest can be bought now for a fourth or fifth part of the sum they would have cost thirty or forty years ago, and, from all appearances, they are likely to decline still further in the market. The great work on this subject is Dibdin's *Rare and Valuable Editions of the Greek and Latin Classics* (2 vols., 1827), which can sometimes be bought by auction for as little as £1.

Art books are so numerous, and so readily subdivided into an infinite number of classes, that they are rarely, if ever, collected as a whole. Amateurs invariably use the *Universal Catalogue of Books on Art*, which was compiled by order of the Lords of the Committee of the Council on Education, and published between the years 1870-7 (in 3 vols. sm. 4to). It is a work that would be exceedingly difficult to improve upon, though as time goes on it will of course be necessary to add to it.

Works on Shorthand are catalogued by J. W. Gibson (Pitman & Sons, 1887), on Magic and Witchcraft in Scribner's *Bibliotheca Diabolica* (New York, 1874), while books on music and all about them are noted in C. Engel's *Literature of National Music* (1879, 8vo).

We now come to the point when a short description of the more modern methods of book collecting becomes a matter of necessity. For some years it has been the fashion to collect not so much works of a certain class as of particular authors, chiefly those which are embellished with plates. By common consent first editions are, with a few exceptions, alone worthy of note; and it is also an axiom that where a book was originally published in parts, those parts must on no account be bound up in volume form. If the collector should be so ill advised as to bind the parts, notwithstanding the decrees of fashion to the contrary, he may save his position no little by binding in the title-pages and also the lists of advertisements, but if he neglects to do this, then his case is hopeless. This is an example of the ridiculous rules which have been laid down by a generation of autocratic book lovers, not one of whom could in all probability give a satisfactory reason for his *dicta*. It is, however, the rule, and will have to be followed, since great pecuniary loss is certain to follow the slightest infraction of it. Although the amateur does not buy his books to sell again, still I apprehend it is a satisfaction to know that, in case he should ever be compelled, though against his will, to sell them, he will be able to do so without losing by his bargain. Original editions of Dickens' works find a ready market, at ever-increasing prices; but in addition to his better-known books, the very titles of which have now become household words, there are others which are not so generally known, such, for example, as the *Curious Dance*, the *Village Coquettes* and many small pieces which are scattered about the pages of the magazines, and are usually classed under the heading *Dickensiana*. The same remarks, but even perhaps to a still greater extent, apply to Thackeray and his works, for that great author worked for many years before his genius became recognised. The bibliographer who has smoothed the way for the Dickens and Thackeray collector is Mr. C. P. Johnson, in his *Hints to Collectors of Original Editions of the Works of Charles Dickens* (1885), and his *Hints to Collectors of Original Editions of the Works of W. M. Thackeray* (1885).

The same author's *Early Writings of William Makepeace Thackeray* (1888) contains a list of all the pieces which can now be identified, and of the places where they are to be found, so as to put it readily in the power of the biographer, the collector, and the student to refer to them if he will. The *Snob, Gownsman, National Omnibus, National Standard, The Constitutional*, and *Fraser's Magazine* all contain essays, articles, or tales from his able pen, which, but for Mr. Johnson's patient efforts, might have been lost in course of time, when the evidence to identify them would have been wanting.

Bibliographies of the works of Carlyle, Swinburne, Ruskin, and Tennyson, as well as those of Dickens and Thackeray, have been compiled by R. H. Shepherd, and of the works of Hazlitt, Leigh Hunt, and Lamb by Alexander Ireland.

That famous artist George Cruikshank illustrated a large number of books, all of which are eagerly sought after by certain bodies of collectors. As in the case of other illustrated books, the value mainly depends upon the earliness of impression of the plates, and the condition; and consequently original editions are more highly esteemed than those which followed. Some capacity for judging engravings is required of the amateur who makes this branch of the subject a speciality, but in other respects he will find almost everything he is likely to require in G. W. Reid's *Descriptive Catalogue of the Works of George Cruikshank* (London, 1871, 8vo).

Bewick collectors have an infallible guide in the Rev. T. Hugo's *Bewick Collector, a Descriptive Catalogue of the Works of T. and J. Bewick* (published, with the supplement, in 2 vols., 1866-8, 8vo). It is related of this author that he once found a battered and ragged specimen of a child's book got up on strong-laid paper by the famous engraver. Only one or two copies are known to exist, as Bewick found the enterprise too expensive to pay, and accordingly discontinued it. The owner of this treasure was an old woman, who had derived her infant ideas of lions and tigers from its well-thumbed leaves, and who refused to part with an old friend, though sorely and even desperately pressed to do so.

How often is the enthusiastic book hunter thwarted when his hopes are on the point of being realised; how often must he succumb to what he may consider to be nothing better than prejudice or obstinacy? This is a question which every amateur learns in time to answer for himself.

CHAPTER III.

PAPER-MAKING—DIFFERENT SIZES OF PAPER—DIFFERENT SIZES OF BOOKS—MEASUREMENTS WATER-MARKS—BOOKS TO CONSULT.

THE mould used by paper-makers is a kind of sieve of an oblong shape, bottomed with the very finest wire strands, all of which run horizontally from end to end. From top to bottom, and about an inch apart, are placed "chain wires," and on the right-hand side of the mould the wire water-mark, which, together with the wire-marks, appears semi-transparent. The reason of this is that both water-mark and wires are slightly raised, and of course the pulp is thinner there than anywhere else. Any ordinary sheet of paper held up to the light will show this, and serve to extra illustrate the following diagram.

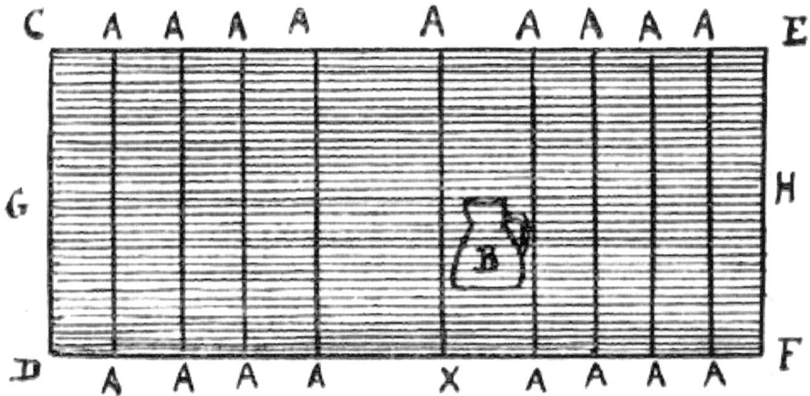

Paper-maker's Mould: Jug Water-mark.

Here CDEF is the mould which the workman drops into a vat of pulp, the fine strands run from G to H all the way down the mould, AA, &c., are the chain wires, and B is the water-mark, in this case a jug. The water in the pulp of course runs through the sieve, leaving a layer of soft matter, which after a while hardens into a sheet of paper. The water-mark was at one time the trade mark of the maker, but subsequently became merely a symbol denoting the size of the sheet of paper before it was folded. The smallest sheet was water-marked with a jug, as above, and termed "pot"; the next had a cap and bells, hence our term "foolscap"; the next a horn, hence "post". Others had a "crown," and so on. At the present day all water-marks have once more become trade symbols, and cannot be depended upon to afford any evidence of size; but at one time—*i.e.*, before the year 1750—this was not so, and, therefore, these water-marks, irrespective of their antiquarian value, serve a useful purpose—namely, to point out in cases of doubt whether any given book is an octavo, quarto, or folio, or a variation of any of these sizes.

To refer once more to the diagram. Take a sheet of paper supposed to have come from the mould and double it in half at the line AX. The water-mark will in that event appear in the centre of the half sheet, and the folded paper is of folio size. Now fold the paper the contrary way, and the water-mark will appear at the bottom, but cut in half; the paper thus folded is quarto (4to). Now fold it the contrary way again, and a section of the water-mark will appear at the top; the paper thus folded is octavo (8vo). We can go on folding, and in every subsequent case the watermark will appear at the edges, while, as the paper gets smaller and smaller, the sizes are styled 12mo, 16mo, 32mo, and so forth.

In the example given, a book made of the sheet of paper in question would be a pot folio, pot 4to, pot 8vo, and so on; but as larger-sized papers were used, another book might be a post 8vo, or a crown 4to, &c., according to circumstances.

As stated, this is one way of finding out the size of an old book; but there is another way—by means of the "signatures," which consist of small letters or figures at the foot of the page of nearly every book. The leaves (not pages) must be counted between signature and signature, and then if there are two leaves the book is a folio, if four a 4to, if eight an 8vo, if twelve a 12mo, if sixteen a 16mo, and if thirty-two a 32mo. Take, as an example, this very book you hold in your hand, and it will be found that there are eight leaves between signature and signature; hence it is an 8vo, though a small one, owing, of course, to the small size of the paper from which it has been made, *viz.*, crown. Had it been a little smaller (still preserving its oblong shape) it would have been a foolscap 8vo, if somewhat larger a demy 8vo, if larger still a royal 8vo, and largest of all imperial 8vo. The quartos and folios are governed by identical rules, and hence in the trade the sizes of books are very numerous.

Simple as this method of computation may appear, a great deal of controversy has taken place on the subject—so much so, indeed, that there are people to be found who stoutly maintain, and adduce proof to show, that what looks like a 4to is in reality an 8vo, or *vice versâ*. It would be out of place to enter into a discussion of this nature, and, therefore, I should advise the young collector to count the leaves between signature and signature, and to abide by the result, regardless of all the learned arguments of specialists. If there are no signatures, and the book is an old one, then study the position of the water-mark.

As examples, it will be sufficient to note that the *Illustrated London News* is folio, *Punch* is 4to, and the *Cornhill* and nearly all the monthly magazines are large 8vos. There is a large number of varieties of each size, but on the whole books which approximate to the sizes of magazines are of the sizes named. Occasionally in judging by the eye in this manner a mistake may be made; but of one thing there is no doubt, that a vast amount of argument would have to be expended upon the subject before the judgment could be proved to be wrong.

Paper-makers at one period made their sheets in frames of a given size, so that it was a comparatively easy matter to distinguish the size of a book at a glance. Now-a-days, however, there appears to be but little uniformity in this respect, and the difficulty is consequently considerably increased. The following measurements will, however, be found approximately correct, and they may be utilised in a practical manner by taking a sheet of brown paper of the required size and folding it as previously mentioned, thus forming crown 8vos, crown 4tos, elephant folios, &c., at will. The practice is good, and it will not need to be often repeated.

A sheet of	foolscap	measures about	17 in. x 13 in.
A sheet of	post	measures about	19 in. x 15 in.
A sheet of	crown	measures about	20 in. x 15 in.
A sheet of	demy	measures about	22 in. x 17 in.
A sheet of	royal	measures about	24 in. x 19 in.
A sheet of	imperial	measures about	30 in. x 22 in.
A sheet of	elephant	measures about	28 in. x 23 in.
A sheet of	atlas	measures about	34 in. x 26 in.

The only paper used, as a general rule, for making up into 8vo books is foolscap, post, crown, demy, royal, and imperial; 4to books are made up of all the sizes; though elephant and atlas are chiefly devoted to folios.

I now take leave of this branch of the subject, and return to water-marks, which, as previously stated, were formerly used, as they are now, for trade marks, and as trade marks only.

Before the year 1320, paper was very rarely used to write upon, but still there are a few examples of it having been so employed extant, the chief of which is an account-book preserved at the Hague, commencing with the year 1301. The water-mark on the paper of this book is a globe surmounted by a cross, while on paper of a little later date the rude representation of a jug frequently appears. The globe and the jug are consequently the most ancient water-marks yet discovered, and these became the principal marks on paper, then exclusively manufactured in Holland and Belgium. The "can and reaping hook" appeared a little later, so did the "two cans," the "open hand," and the "half *fleur-de-lis*," all executed, as might be expected, in the rudest possible manner.

The Holbein family at Ravensburg—a town famous to this day for the manufacture of paper—used a "bull's head". Fust and Schœffer (*circa* 1460) used a "clapper" or rattle, which has a somewhat curious history. At Ravensburg there was an hospital for lepers, and whenever any of the inmates had occasion to leave the building he was strictly enjoined to flourish a rattle with which he was provided, so that healthy folk could get out of his way. Paper made at the town is often found marked with the rattle, that having grown, by reason of its frequent use, into an institution of the place.

The next marks in point of date are in all probability the "unicorn," "anchor," and the "P" and "Y," the initials of Philip of Burgundy and his wife Isabella, who were married in 1430.

The famous English printer Caxton (*c.* A.D. 1424-91)[4] used the "bull's head" paper from Ravensburg, the "P" and "Y," the "open hand," and the "unicorn"; sometimes even the "bunch of grapes," which came from Italy.

The first folio of Shakespeare's works (1623) has paper marked with a "fool's cap" among other devices. The "post horn," another favourite device, which has given the name to a particular size of paper—namely, "post"—was first used about the year 1670, when the General Post Office was established, and it became the fashion for the postman to blow a horn.

In modern times paper-marks have become so numerous that it would be next to impossible to classify them; nor would it be of much advantage to the book collector even if it could be done. With old marks it is different, for *fac-simile* reprints of scarce and ancient volumes are frequently detected by looking at the water-mark on the paper. Of course, this also may be imitated, but there is often considerable difficulty in attaining the requisite degree of perfection; and, under any circumstance, some little knowledge of the early history and appearance of water-marks will be found useful as well as interesting. The best books to consult on the subject are Herring's *Paper and Papermaking* and Sotheby's *Principia Typographica*, 1858, the latter of which is a masterpiece of learning and constructive skill.

---

[4] It is very improbable that Caxton was born in 1412, as nearly all his biographers state, but about ten or twelve years later. Evidence of this is contained in the records preserved at Mercers' Hall, Cheapside, London, where his name is inscribed as having been apprenticed in the year 1438, the age at which apprenticeship was entered upon being most commonly between twelve and fourteen years.

CHAPTER IV.

IT must be borne in mind that the title-page of a book, though constituting a very old method of showing at a glance the nature of the contents, together with the place of publication and frequently also the date, is by no means the earliest means of attaining that object. The title-page, such as we see it, was first adopted in England in 1490, the year before Caxton's death, having been introduced on the Continent in 1470;[5] but previously—and, indeed, for some years after that date—the *Colophon* was in general use.

The term "Colophon" has its origin in the Greek proverb, "to put the colophon to the matter," that is, the "finishing stroke," and contains the place or year (or both), date of publication, printer's name, and other particulars considered necessary at the time for the identification of the volume. It frequently commences somewhat after the following form: *Explicit liber qui dicitur*, &c.[6] The colophon, moreover, is always found on the last page, and sometimes takes the form of an inverted pyramid. In the early days, when the printer was not unfrequently author or translator as well, the completion of a work upon which he had probably been engaged for many months—or, perhaps, in some instances, years—was rightly regarded as matter for much self-congratulation, as well as for thanks to the Divine Power, by whose permission alone he had been enabled to persevere. Hence the *Psalterium* of Fust and Schœffer, a folio of 175 lines to the page, and remarkable as being the first book in which large capital letters, printed in colours, were employed, has for its colophon a very characteristic inscription, which may be translated as follows:—

"This book of Psalms, decorated with antique initials and sufficiently emphasised with rubricated letters, has been thus made by the masterly invention of printing and also type-making, without the writing of a pen, and is consummated to the service of God through the industry of Johann Fust, citizen of Mentz, and Peter Schœffer, of Gernsheim, in the year of our Lord MCCCCLVII., on the eve of the Assumption".

This Psalter is also the first known book which bears any date at all, and for

---

[5] *Vide* Pollard's *Last Words on the History of the Title-page* (Lond., 1891).

[6] Some recent French publishers, such as Quantin and Rouveyre, have imitated the practice in their editions for bibliophiles.

that and other reasons is one of the most highly prized of volumes.

From what has been said, the reader will no doubt clearly understand that it does not follow that, because an old book is minus a title-page, it is necessarily imperfect. He should turn to the last leaf for the colophon; but should that be wanting also, it is probable that the book is deficient, though even this is not a conclusive test. In cases of doubt the volume must be *collated*, that is, critically compared with some other specimen: each leaf must be examined carefully, and notes made of any differences that may appear during the course of the examination. There is a business-like way and the reverse of tabulating these notes, so much so that an adept can see at a glance whether it has been performed by a competent man. The following is the collation of a copy of the first edition of the famous Genevan version of the Bible printed by Rowland Hall in 1560, 4to: "Four prel. leaves. Text, Genesis to ii. Maccabees, 474 ll. folioed, N. T. 122 leaves, 'A Briefe Table' HH h iii to LLl iii., 13 ll. followed by 1 p. 'The order of the yeres from Paul's conversion,' &c., rev. blank."

At first sight this may appear somewhat technical, but when a few of these collations are compared with actual copies of the works to which they refer, there will be no difficulty in understanding all the rest. The above, for instance, would read, when set out at full length, as follows: "There are four preliminary leaves, and then follows the Bible text proper, which, from Genesis to the 2nd of Maccabees, is on 474 numbered leaves. The New Testament, which follows, has 122 leaves; then comes 'A Briefe Table,' extending from signature HH h iii to LL l iii, and comprising 13 leaves, followed by one page, 'The order of the yeres from Paul's conversion,' &c. The reverse side of this page is blank." The words "page" and "leaf" have distinct meanings, the latter, of course, containing two of the former, unless, indeed, one side happens to be blank, as in the above example. If both sides are blank, the description would be simply "i 1 blank".

From 1457—the date of Fust and Schœffer's Psalter, already described as being the first printed book disclosing on its face the year of publication—until comparatively recent times, it was customary to use Roman numerals on the colophon or title-page, as the case might be. This system of notation is so well understood, or can be so speedily mastered from almost any arithmetical treatise, that it is hardly worth while to enlarge upon it here. On some old books, however, there is a dual form of the "D" representing 500, which is sometimes the cause of considerable perplexity; e.g., MIƆXL standing for the year 1540. In this example the I is equivalent to D; in fact, it would appear as if the former numeral were merely a mutilation of the latter. Again, the form CIƆ is equivalent to M or 1000. A few instances will make the distinction apparent:—

$$\left.\begin{array}{l} \text{M I}\!\supset\text{ XXIV} \\ \text{or M D XXIV} \end{array}\right\} = 1524; \qquad \left.\begin{array}{l} \text{CI}\!\supset\text{ I}\!\supset\text{ CLXXXV} \\ \text{or M D CLXXXVIII} \end{array}\right\} = 1685;$$

$$\left.\begin{array}{l} \text{CI}\!\supset\text{ I}\!\supset\text{ CLXXXV} \\ \text{or M D CLXXXV} \end{array}\right\} = 1661;$$

The only part of a title-page which gives any real difficulty to a person who has a fair knowledge of the Latin language, in which most of these old books were printed, is the name of the place of publication, which, being in a Latinised form, frequently bears but a slight resemblance to the modern appellation. Dr. Cotton, many years ago now, collected a large number of these Latin forms, partly from his own reading and partly from the works of various bibliographers who had chanced occasionally to mention them in their works, and at the present day his collection stands unapproachable in point of the number of entries, as well as in general accuracy. The use of this compilation will be apparent to those who have occasion to consult it even for the first time, while to advanced collectors, who are not satisfied with mere possession, it will be found indispensable. The title-page of a book now before me runs as follows: *"Kanuti Episcopi Vibergensis Quedam breves expositõs s legum et jurium cõcordantie et allegatiões circa leges iucie"*; at the foot is "Ripis, M. Brand, MIƆIIII". The question immediately arises: Where is Ripis, the place where the book was evidently printed by Brand? The best gazetteer may be consulted in vain, for the title is obsolete now; it is, in fact, the Roman name for Riben, a small place in Denmark. In like manner, Firenze frequently stands for Florence, Brixia for Breschia, Aug. Trinob. (Augusta Trinobantum) for London, Mutina for Modena, and so on. This being the case, some kind of tabulation becomes absolutely necessary, and the best that occurs to my mind is to place the Latin titles of all the chief centres of printing in alphabetical order, and append to each the English equivalent. The date is that of the first book known to have been printed at the particular town against which it is set. As the list is not complete, and could not be made so without the sacrifice of a great deal of space, the reader is referred to Dr. Cotton's *Typographical Antiquities* for any further information he may require. The omissions will be found, however, to consist, for the most part, of unimportant places, from many of which only some half-dozen books or less are known to have been issued, so that the following list will be found sufficient in the vast majority of cases:—

1486.	Abbatis Villa	Abbeville.
1621.	Abredonia	Aberdeen.
1493.	Alba	Acqui (in Italy).
1480.	Albani Villa	St. Albans.
1501.	Albia	Albia (in Savoy).
1480.	Aldenarda	Oudenarde.
1473.	Alostum	Alost (in Flanders).
1467.	Alta Villa	Eltville, or Elfeld (near Mayence).
1523.	Amstelœdamum	Amsterdam.
1476.	Andegavum	Angers.
	Aneda	Edinburgh.
1491.	Angolismum	Angoulême.
1482.	Antverpia	Antwerp.
1482.	Aquila	Aquila (near Naples).

1456(?).	Argentina, or Argentoratum	Strassburg.
1477.	Asculum	Ascoli (in Ancona).
1474.	Athenæ Rauracæ	Basle.
1517.	Atrebatum	Arras.
1469.	Augusta Vindelicorum	Augsburg.
1480.	Augusta Trinobantum	London.
1481.	Auracum	Urach (in Wurtemberg).
1490.	Aurelia	Orleans.
1490.	Aureliacum	Orleans.
1497.	Avenio	Avignon.
1462.	Bamberga	Bamberg.
1478.	Barchine	Barcelona.
1497.	Barcum	Barco (in Italy).
1474.	Basilea	Basle.
1470.	{Berona, or Beronis Villa }	Beron Minster (in Switzerland).
1487.	Bisuntia	Besançon.
1471.	Bononia	Bologna.
1485.	Bravum Burgi	Burgos.
1472.	Brixia	Breschia.
1475.	Brugæ	Bruges.
1486.	Brunna	Brunn.
1476.	Bruxellæ	Brussels.
1473.	Buda	Buda.
1485.	Burgi	Burgos.
1484.	Buscum Ducis	Bois-le-duc.
1478.	Cabelia	Chablies (in France).
1480.	Cadomum	Caen.
1475.	Cæsar Augusta, or Caragoça	Saragossa.
1484.	Camberiacum	Chambery.
1521.	Cantabrigia	Cambridge.
1497.	Carmagnola	Carmagnola.
1622.	Carnutum	Chartres.
1494.	Carpentoratum	Carpentras.
1486.	Casale Major	Casal-Maggiore.
1475.	Cassela	Caselle (in Piedmont).
1484.	Chamberium	Chambery.

1482.	Coburgum	Coburg.
1466.	Colonia	Cologne.
1466.	Colonia Agrippina	Cologne.
1466.	Colonia Claudia	Cologne.
1460.	Colonia Munatiana	Basle.
1466.	Colonia Ubiorum	Cologne.
1474.	Comum	Como.
1516.	Conimbrica	Coimbra.
1505.	Constantia	Constance.
1487.	Cordova	Cordova.
1469.	Coria	Soria (in Old Castile).
1500 (about).	Cracovia	Cracow (Poland).
1472.	Cremona	Cremona.
1480.	Culemburgum	Culembourg (in Holland).
1478.	Cusentia	Cosenza.
1475.	Daventria	Deventer (in Holland).
1477.	Delphi	Delft.
1491.	Divio	Dijon.
1490.	Dola	Dol (in France).
1564.	Duacum	Douay.
	Eblana	Dublin.
1509.	Eboracum	York.
	Edemburgum	Edinburgh.
1440(?).	Elvetrorum Argentina	Strassburg.
1491.	Engolismum	Angoulême.
1482.	Erfordia	Erfurt.
1472.	Essium	Jesi (in Italy).
1473.	Esslinga	Esslingen (in Wurtemberg).
1531.	Ettelinga	Etlingen.
1471.	Ferrara	Ferrara.
1471.	Firenze	Florence.
1472.	Fivizanum	Fivzziano (in Tuscany).
1471.	Florentia	Florence.
1495.	Forum Livii	Forli (in Italy).
1504.	Francofurtum ad Mœnum	Frankfort on the Maine.
1504.	Francofortum ad Oderam	Frankfort on the Oder.

1495.	Frisinga	Freysingen.
1470.	Fulgineum	Foligno (in Italy).
1487.	Gaietta	Gaeta.
1490.	Ganabum	Orleans.
1483.	Gandavvm, or Gand	Ghent.
1478.	Geneva	Geneva.
1474.	Genua	Genoa.
1483.	Gerunda	Gerona (in Spain).
1477.	Gouda	Gouda.
1490.	Gratianopolis	Grenoble.
1493.	Hafnia	Copenhagen.
	Haga Comitum	The Hague.
1491.	Hamburgum	Hamburg.
1491.	Hamnionia	Hamburg.
1483.	Harlemum (probably earlier date)	Haarlem.
1504.	Helenopolis	Frankfort on the Maine.
1479.	Herbipolis	Wurtzburg.
1476.	Hispalis, or Colonia Julia Romana	Seville.
1483.	Holmia	Stockholm.
1487.	Ingolstadium	Ingolstadt.
1473.	Lauginga	Laugingen (in Bavaria).
1483.	Leida	Leyden.
1495.	Lemovicense Castrum	Limoges.
1566.	Leodium	Liège.
1503.	Leucorea	Wittemburg.
1480.	Lipsia	Leipsic.
1485.	Lixboa	Lisbon.
1474(?).	Londinum	London.
1474.	Lovanium	Louvain.
1475.	Lubeca	Lubec.
1477.	Luca	Lucca.
1473.	Lugdunum	Lyons.
1483.	Lugdunum Batavorum	Leyden.
1499.	Madritum	Madrid.

1483.	Magdeburgum	Magdeburg.
1442(?).	Maguntia	Mayence.
1732.	Mancunium	Manchester.
1472.	Mantua	Mantua.
1527.	Marpurgum	Marburg.
1473.	Marsipolis	Mersburg.
1493.	Matisco	Mâcon.
1470.	Mediolanum	Milan.
1473.	Messana	Messina.
1500.	Monachium	Munich.
1470.	Monasterium	Munster (in Switzerland).
1472.	Mons Regalis	Mondovi (in Piedmont).
1475.	Mutina	Modena.
1510.	Nanceium	Nancy.
1471.	Neapolis	Naples.
1493.	Nannetes	Nantes.
1525.	Nerolinga	Nordlingen (in Suabia).
1480.	Nonantula	Nonantola (in Modena).
1469.	Norimberga	Nuremberg.
1479.	Novi	Novi (near Genoa).
1479.	Noviomagium	Nimeguen.
1533.	Neocomum	Neuchatel.
1494.	Oppenhemium	Oppenheim.
1468.	Oxonia	Oxford (the date is disputed).
1477.	Panormum	Palermo.
1471.	Papia	Pavia.
1470.	Parisii	Paris.
1472.	Parma	Parma.
1481.	Patavia	Passau (in Bavaria).
1472.	Patavium	Padua.
1475.	Perusia	Perugia.
1479.	Pictavium	Poitiers.
1483.	Pisa	Pisa.
1472.	Plebisacium	Piobe de Sacco (in Italy).
1478.	Praga	Prague.
1495.	Ratiastum Lemovicum	Limoges.

1485.	Ratisbona	Ratisbon.
1480.	Regium	Reggio.
1482.	Reutlinga	Reutlingen.
1484.	Rhedones	Rennes.
1503.	Ripa or Ripis	Ripen (in Denmark).
1467.	Roma	Rome.
1487.	Rothomagum	Rouen.
1479.	Saena	Siena.
1480.	Salmantice	Salamanca.
1470.	Savillianum	Savigliano (in Piedmont).
1474.	Savona	Savona.
1483.	Schedamum	Schiedam.
1479.	Senæ	Siena.
1484.	Soncino	Soncino (Italy).
1514.	Southwark	Southwark.
1471.	Spira	Spires (in Pavaria).
1465.	Sublacense Monasterium. An independent monastery about two miles distant from Subiaco, in the Campagna di Roma.	
1484.	Sylva Ducis	Bois-le-duc.
1471.	Tarvisium	Treviso (in Italy).
1474.	Taurinum	Turin.
1468.	Theatrum Sheldonianum (the date is disputed)	Oxford.
1521.	Tigurum	Zurich.
1479.	Tholosa	Toulouse.
1480.	Toletum	Toledo.
1473.	Trajectum ad Rhenum	Utrecht.
1504.	Trajectum ad Viadrum	Frankfort on the Oder.
1471.	Trajectum Inferius	Utrecht.
1470.	Trebia	Trevi (in Italy).
1483.	Trecæ	Troyes.
1440 (?).	Tribboccorum	Strassburg.
1483.	Tricasses	Troyes.
1476.	Tridentum Trent (in the Tyrol).	
1498.	Tubinga	Tübingen.

1521.	Turigum	Zurich.
1496.	Turones	Tours.
1479.	Tusculanum	Toscolano (in Italy).
1471(?).	Ulma	Ulm.
1471.	Ultrajectum	Utrecht.
1485.	Ulyssipo	Lisbon.
1481.	Urbinum	Urbino.
1474.	Valentia	Valentia.
1474.	Vallis S. Mariæ	Marienthal (an Augustine monastery near Mentz, now suppressed).
1469.	Venetiæ	Venice.
1485.	Vercellæ	Vercelli.
1470.	Verona	Verona.
1487.	Vesontio	Besançon.
1473.	Vicentia	Vicenza.
1517.	Vilna	Wilna (in Russia).
1482.	Vindobona	Vienna.
1503.	Vitemberga	Wittemburg.
1488.	Viterbium	Viterbo.
	Vratislavia	Breslau.
1474.	Westmonasterium	Westminster.
1475.	Wirceburgum	Wurtzburg.

CHAPTER V.

THE REASONS WHICH MAKE A BOOK VALUABLE—SCARCI-
TY— SUPPRESSED WORKS—SOME BOOKS WHICH HAVE
BEEN BURNED BY THE HANGMAN—WORKS PRIVATELY
SUPPRESSED—WORKS OF LIMITED ISSUE—TRANSACTIONS
OF LEARNED SOCIETIES—DEFECTS—"UNCUT" WORKS—
IMPERFECT COPIES—"MADE-UP" COPIES—FAC-SIMILE
LEAVES—LAYING DOWN—BOOKS PUBLISHED IN PARTS—
LARGE-PAPER COPIES.

THE reasons which contribute to make up the pecuniary value of a book depend on a variety of circumstances by no means easy of explanation. It is a great mistake to suppose that because a given work is scarce, in the sense of not often being met with, it is necessarily valuable. It may certainly be so, but, on the other hand, plenty of books which are acquired with difficulty are hardly worth the paper they are printed upon, perhaps because there is no demand for them, or possibly because they are imperfect or mutilated.

One of the first lessons I learned when applying myself to the study of old books was never, on any account or under any circumstances, to have anything to do with imperfect copies, and I have not so far had any occasion to regret my decision. It is perfectly true that no perfect copies are known of some works, such, for example, as the first or 1562-3 English edition of Fox's *Book of Martyrs*; but books of this class will either never be met with during a lifetime, or will form, if met with, an obvious exception to the rule. Fragments of genuine Caxtons, again, sometimes sell by auction for two or three pounds a single leaf, and even a very imperfect copy of any of his productions would be considered a good exchange for a large cheque; but these are exceptions and nothing more— exceptions, moreover, of such rare practical occurrence as to be hardly worth noting. In the vast majority of instances, when a book is mutilated it is ruined; even the loss of a single plate out of many will often detract fifty per cent. or more from the normal value, while if the book is "cut down" the position is worse. This lesson as a rule is only learned by experience, and many young collectors resolutely shut their eyes to the most apparent of truisms, until such time as the consequences are brought fairly home to them. It is exceedingly dangerous to purchase imperfect or mutilated books, or to traffic in them at all. This position will be enlarged upon during the progress of the present chapter.

To return to the reasons which contribute to the value of a book, it may be mentioned that "suppression" is one of the chief. This is a natural reason; others are merely artificial, which may be in full force to-day but non-existent to-morrow, depending as they do upon mere caprice and the vagaries of fashion: with these I have, in this volume at any rate, nothing to do.

De Foe, in his *Essay on Projects*, observes: "I have heard a bookseller in King James's time say that if he would have a book sell, he would have it burned by the hands of the common hangman," by which he presupposed the existence of some little secret horde which should escape the general destruction, and which would consequently rise to ten times its value directly the persecution was diverted into other channels. This is so, for where an edition has been suppressed, and most of the copies destroyed, the remainder acquire an importance which the whole issue would never have enjoyed had it been left severely alone. The Inquisition has been the direct cause of elevating hundreds of books to a position far above their merit, and the same may be said of Henry VIII., who sent Catholic as well as Protestant books wholesale to the flames; of Mary, who condemned the latter; of Edward VI., who acquiesced in the destruction of the former; and of Elizabeth and the two succeeding sovereigns, who delighted in a holocaust of political pamphlets and libels.

The Inquisition, with that brutal bigotry which characterised most of its proceedings, almost entirely destroyed Grafton's Paris Bible of 1538, with the result that the printing presses, types, and workmen were brought to London, and the few copies saved were completed here, to be sold on rare occasions at the present day for as much as £160 apiece. There is nothing in the Bible more than in any other; it is not particularly well printed, but it has a history, just as the Scotch Bassandyne Bible has, though in that case the persecution was directed against persons who *declined* to have the book in their houses, ready to be shown to the tax collector whenever he chose to call. One Dr. James Drake, who in the year 1703 had the temerity to publish in London his *Historia Anglo-Scotica*, which contained, as was alleged, many false and injurious reflections upon the sovereignty and independence of the Scottish nation, had the pleasure of hearing that his work had been publicly burned at the Mercat Cross of Edinburgh, a pleasure which was doubtless considerably enhanced when another venture—the *Memorial*—shared the same fate in London, two years later. Drake had the honour of hearing himself censured from the throne, of being imprisoned, and of having his books burned, distinctions which some people sigh for in vain at the present day. As a consequence, the *Historia* and the *Memorial* are both desirable books, and Drake's name has been rescued from oblivion.

William Attwood's *Superiority and Direct Dominion of the Imperial Crown of England over the Crown and Kingdom of Scotland* (London, 4to, 1705) is another book of good pedigree which would never have been worth the couple of guineas a modern bookseller will ask for it, had it not been burned by jealous Scotchmen immediately on its appearance.

The massacre of St. Bartholomew produced a large crop of treatises, and any contemporary book on the Huguenot side is worth preservation, for a general search was made throughout France, and every work showing the slightest favour to the Protestants was seized and destroyed. Among them was Claude's *Défense de la Réformation* (1683), which was burned not only abroad, but in England as well, so great an ascendency had the French Ambassador acquired over our Court.

Bishop Burnet's *Pastoral letter to the Clergy of his Diocese* (1689) was condemned and burned for ascribing the title of William III. to the Crown, to the right of conquest. The *Emilie* and the *Contrat Social* of Jean Jacques Rousseau shared the same fate, as did also *Les Histoires* of d'Aubigné and Augustus de Thou.

Baxter's *Holy Commonwealth* went the way of all obnoxious books, in 1688; the *Boocke of Sportes upon the Lord's Day*, in 1643; the Duke of Monmouth's proclamation declaring James to be an usurper, in 1685; Claude's *Les Plaintes des Protestans*, in 1686.

Harris' *Enquiry into the Causes of the Miscarriage of the Scots Colony at Darien* (Glasgow, 1700); Bastwicke's *Elenchus Religionis Papisticæ* (1634); Blount's *King William and Queen Mary, Conquerors, &c.* (1692); the second volume of Wood's *Athenæ Oxoniensis* (1793); De Foe's *Shortest Way with the Dissenters* (1702); Pocklington's *Sunday no Sabbath and Altare Christianum* (1640); Sacheverel's *Two Sermons* (1710); and Coward's *Second Thoughts concerning the Human Soul* (1702), were all burned by the hangman, and copies destroyed wherever found.

Perhaps the most extraordinary instance of a work being destroyed for positively nothing at all is furnished by Cowell's *Law Dictionary*, which was sent to the flames by order of King James the First himself. This dictionary, and indeed every one of the books mentioned as having been subjected to the purification of fire, are now rare historical landmarks, and consequently both extrinsically and intrinsically valuable. Hence the reason of the high prices frequently demanded for them and for other works of this class.

The remaining copies of editions which were suppressed by their authors, or which have escaped accidental destruction, are frequently of considerable value. In the former class, Rochester's *Poems* and Mrs. Seymour's *Account of the Origin of the Pickwick Papers* are prominent examples; in the latter, the third folio edition of Shakespeare's Plays (1664), almost the entire impression of which was destroyed in the Great Fire of London. Dugdale's *Origines Juridiciales* (London, folio, 1666) was also almost entirely destroyed at the same time. Books coming under one or other of these classes are to be met with, and the note-book should always be at hand, so that a memorandum can be jotted down before the reference is lost. This course is adopted by the most experienced bibliographers, as well as by the amateur who wishes to become proficient in a study which is pleasant and profitable when conscientiously undertaken, but difficult and worse than useless to those who will not take the trouble to learn the rudiments of their science.

Works of limited issue are sometimes, but not always, nor indeed often, of especial value. It has been the practice for some years among publishers to issue works on what is nothing more nor less than the old subscription plan; but, unlike the hungry poets of old, who trudged the streets taking the price of copies in advance, the publishers keep faith with their subscribers. The edition is limited to a given number of copies, after which the type is distributed, and the plates—if the work is illustrated—broken up. Many speculators in books have endeavoured from time to time to "corner" editions so limited in quantity, buying at the published price, and subsequently selling again at an increased amount. In this way considerable sums have been *lost*, for works published on this plan have a decided tendency to fall in the market, and when this is the case they seldom if ever recover their former position. Hogarth's works, published in 1822, by Baldwin and Cradock, is a very good example of this tendency. The work was originally issued at £50, and the impressions, taken from Hogarth's original plates, restored, however, by Heath, are consequently of full size. There is a secret pocket at the end containing three suppressed and highly indecent plates, which considerably add to the value. I myself have many a time seen this large and sumptuous book knocked down in the auction room at sums varying from £3 to £5, and once bought a good copy by private contract for £4 10s. Ottley's *Italian School of Design* is another example. This work when on large paper, with proof impressions of the 84 tinted fac-similes of original drawings by Cimabue, Giotto, Guercino, and other famous painters, is worth about £3 by auction. The published price in 1823 was no less than £25 4s. The issue of each of these works was limited, but neither have succeeded in retaining its position in popular favour, and in all probability will decline still further in the market as time goes on.

The lesson to be learned here is that such phrases as "only 100 copies printed," or "issue strictly limited to 50 copies," frequently to be observed in publishers' and auctioneers' catalogues, should be taken *cum grano salis*. The description may be accurate, but it does not follow that the limitation necessarily increases the value of the book. On the contrary, it may be well imagined that the publisher hesitated to launch the book entirely on its own merits, seeking rather the extraneous inducement of a "limited number". The earlier editions of Ruskin's works are an exception to the rule, for that author's reputation is deservedly great, and he is, moreover, master of his own books, which from choice he has, until the last year or two, preferred to render difficult of access.

Volumes of transactions and proceedings of learned societies usually have a market value, which fluctuates much less than is usually the case. These being supplied to members only, and rarely published for purposes of sale, may be said to be both privately printed and limited in issue at the same time. As a rule they increase proportionately in value as the series becomes more complete, and a point once reached, they generally maintain it. Hence works of this character are safe investments — perhaps the safest of any.

The result of every investigation into the causes which regulate the value of books has shown conclusively that no publication is of great worth merely *because* it is scarce. The scarcity is a secondary and not a primary cause. Highly appreciated English publications of the sixteenth and two following centuries may be counted by thousands; but the number of inferior treatises, which have long ago sunk into eternal oblivion, which never were of any value, and never will be, are as the sand on the sea-shore.

However scarce and valuable a book may be, it must be remembered that the element of perfection has yet to be taken into account. It does not by any means follow that, because a copy of one of Shakespeare's 4tos is worth £300, another copy of the same 4to edition will be of equal value. It may be worth more or less, and here it is that the critical eye of the *connoisseur* and dealer tells. Defects, such as a tear in the cover or any of the leaves, stains, worm-holes, and the like, detract from the value; if these are entirely absent, the value may, on the contrary, be raised above the average. The fact of a rare book being "uncut," and in the original sound binding, clean, and free from blemishes, considerably add to its value.

The first part of a book to get worn out is the binding, for some one or more of its previous owners are almost certain to have ill-treated it either by bending the covers until they crack, or by leaving the work exposed to the rain and damp. When the volume is coverless, and usually not before, it will have been re-bound, and the binder will, in ninety-nine cases out of every hundred, have trimmed the edges, that is to say, planed them smooth with a machine he has for the purpose. Sometimes he will have cut as much as half-an-inch from the top, and nearly as much from the other edges; on other occasions, he may have been more merciful; but the result is the same, the book is damaged beyond hope of redemption, and the only question is as to the extent of the injury. The term "uncut," so often seen in catalogues, is, therefore, a technical term, meaning that the edges are left in the same condition as they were when the book was originally issued. It does not mean that the leaves are "not cut open," as so many people appear to think, but simply that the binder, with a fine sense of what is due to a volume of importance, has for once kept his shears in his pocket. The value of a book which has been cut is reduced to an extent proportionate to the quantum of injury inflicted: from 50 to 75 per cent. is the usual reduction, but many works are altogether destroyed. If a scarce book is sent to be re-bound, the binder should have the clearest instructions, in writing, that he is not to trim the edges. Should he do so, notwithstanding the direction, a by no means impossible contingency, he will do it at his own risk, and can be made to suffer the consequences.

Imperfect volumes are always a source of great inconvenience to the collector. First-class bookselling firms will not allow an imperfect book to leave their hands without notice to the purchaser, and, as a consequence, they charge a higher price than would be the case if the latter exercised his own judgment. There are mutual advantages to be gained in dealing with first-class people, for, if a mistake is made on one side or the other, there is usually no difficulty in rectifying it afterwards. Fine old crusted book-worms of the John Hill Burton type prefer, however, to exercise their own discretion in these matters, looking upon that as no inconsiderable part of the pleasure to be derived from the pursuit of their favourite occupation. They do not care to pay for being taught, at least not directly, and make it part of their business to find out for themselves whether a copy offered for sale is perfect or the reverse. As each page is usually numbered, there is no difficulty in ascertaining whether any are missing; not so with the plates, for, unless there is an index to these, the loss of one or two may hardly be noticed until the book comes to be collated with another copy known to be complete. This is a risk which the book buyer has to run, though, as a matter of practice, he protects himself when the purchase is an expensive one, and the dealer a man of credit.

In buying books at a cheap rate, or, in other words, when making a bargain either at a shop or an ordinary street-stall, the purchaser will have to observe the maxim, "Caveat emptor," and it will probably not be until he arrives home with his treasure under his arm that he will have the satisfaction of ascertaining that his bargain is a real one, or the mortification of adding another imperfect book to the long row already on his shelf.

Imperfect books are frequently what is called "made up," that is, completed from other copies, themselves imperfect in other respects. One complete book is worth more than two incomplete ones, and many desirable specimens, in the public libraries and elsewhere, are made up so well that it is frequently impossible to detect the hand of the renovator.

So long as all the leaves of a made-up book are of the same measurement, there would not seem to be much objection to this practice, but there certainly is when the paper of the interpolated leaves is different from the rest, or smaller in size, which it will be if cut down by the binder. Great care must be taken to see that neither of these defects is present, especially when, from the value of a book offered for sale, it may have been worth anyone's while to perfect it.

Another point to be observed in the purchase of very expensive and valuable works is, that none of the leaves have been fac-similed. These fac-similes are done by hand, and frequently so well that they cannot be detected without the aid of a strong glass. The late Henry Stevens tells a good story of a customer of his—Mr. Lenox, of New York, the founder of the Lenox Library, and a most indefatigable collector up to the last hour of his life. "Mr. Lenox was," says Stevens, "principled against raffles, wagers, lotteries, and games of chance generally, but I once led him into a sort of bet in this way, by which I won from him £4. I had acquired a fair copy of that gem of rare books, the quarto edition of *Hariot's Briefe and True Report of the New Found Land of Virginea* (London, Feb., 1588), wanting four leaves in the body of the book. These I had very skilfully traced by Harris, transferred to stone, printed off on old paper of a perfect match, the book and these leaves sized and coloured alike, and bound in morocco by Bedford. The volume was then sent to Mr. Lenox to be examined by him *de visu*, the price to be £25; but, if he could detect the four fac-simile leaves, and would point them out to me without error, the price was to be reduced to £21. By the first post, after the book was received, he remitted me the 20 guineas, with a list of the fac-similes, but on my informing him that two of *his* fac-similes were originals, he immediately remitted the four pounds, and acknowledged his defeat."

This Harris, whose name is prominently mentioned, was probably the greatest adept at this species of imitation who ever lived, and many important but defective works, now in the British Museum, left his hands, to all appearance, in first-rate order and condition.

"Laying down" is a technical term used to express the process of re-backing a torn plate or engraving. Many of the Shakespeare folios have the portrait and verses by Ben Jonson laid down or "re-laid," as the catalogues generally describe it. This, of course, can be detected at a glance, and it may be stated positively that a laid-down plate, frontispiece, or title is looked upon as a serious blemish, inferior only to the entire absence of one or more of the three.

Worm-holes, stains, fox-marks, and other flaws also detract from value; but as many of these may be removed by a judicious application of proper remedies, a special chapter will be reserved for their consideration. The market value of a book is thus composed of many elements, the chief of which is "condition" — above all things, a broad margin, and next, to that, leaves of spotless white.

I have already stated that where editions of the works of famous modern authors containing plates were originally issued in parts, such parts should, on no account, be bound up in volume form. The result of such a course cannot be better illustrated than by taking the well-known *Pickwick Papers* as our example, and studying the following prices, all realised at auction quite recently:—

Posthumous Papers of the Pickwick Club, original ed., with illustrations by Seymour & Browne, and the Buss plates, *complete in numbers*, 1837, 8vo, £8 10s.; £12 14s.; £8 10s.; £6 5s.; £11 5s.

Posthumous Papers of the Pickwick Club, original ed. (*bound*), with illustrations by Seymour & Browne, and the Buss plates, 1837, 8vo, £1 (half calf), £1 1s. (half calf), £3 (calf extra), £2 12s. (half morocco extra), £2 5s. (half calf extra), £1 7s. (half morocco extra), £3 10s. (calf, gilt, an unusually clean copy, recently sold at the Mackenzie sale). The evidence furnished by these quotations is conclusive, and illustrates the principle better than anything else can do, that, in the present state of the English book market, it is the height of folly to bind up original parts of this nature. If, however, it must be done, the depreciation in value may be reduced to a minimum by binding in the best style, and taking care that not only all the covers, but even the pages of advertisements, are bound up also. On no account must the edges be cut, or in any way tampered with, or the value will sink from pounds to shillings on the instant.

I shall conclude this chapter by calling attention to the expression "large paper," so often noticed. It has been the practice for many years, on publishing certain classes of books, to print off a limited number of copies on "large paper," or paper of a larger size than that used for the ordinary copies. Thus, the second edition of Bewick's *Birds*, in 2 vols., 1804, is found in no less than three sizes, ordinary copies in demy 8vo, large paper copies in royal 8vo, and largest paper in imperial 8vo. The text is in each instance precisely the same, but the books themselves are larger in size as we ascend the scale. The well-known *Badminton Library* of sports and pastimes is printed in two sizes, and as large paper copies are invariably limited in number, their value is always greater than that of their more humble brethren. Whether they maintain their original published value is another question which can only be solved by reference to particular cases as and when they arise.

CHAPTER VI.

THE RENOVATION OF BOOKS—DAMP—GREASE MARKS—SUR-
FACE STAINS—BOOK WORMS AND OTHER PESTS.

THE great enemy of books is unquestionably damp, which corrodes the paper, covering it with reddish brown spots, or, in extreme cases, patches. These unsightly marks, if once they have taken a firm hold, cannot be removed, and the most that can be hoped for is some preventive against an aggravation of the evil. Damp, unlike mere surface stains, attacks the tissue of the paper, rotting it completely through, and not infrequently destroying it altogether. It is like a vital disease which insinuates itself into the very seat of life, and, with more or less despatch, consumes its victim.

Unslaked lime, as is well known, has a strong affinity for moisture of every kind, and when there is plenty of this substance about, damp is irresistibly attracted to it. Small saucers full of lime should therefore be placed in close proximity to valuable books, on the shelves if necessary, but never in immediate contact with the books themselves, or the remedy will be as bad as the disease to be guarded against. The action of lime upon moisture has been very well known for centuries, yet no one seems to have thought of applying it to this useful purpose, and books have been doomed to slow but sure destruction for the want of a precaution as simple as it is obvious. Only the other day a correspondent, writing to an American bibliographical journal, pointed out what he called a new remedy against damp, which turned out to be based upon nothing else than the well-known relationship which exists between lime and water. If damp has only just commenced its attack, the part affected should first be touched with a wash of spirits of wine, and when dry with a very weak solution of oxalic acid. If the "fox spots," as they are called, do not then disappear, the injury is permanent and no remedy exists, as far as we at present know.

A really valuable book which stands in need of a thorough cleaning should be placed in the hands of some competent person, as considerable experience is necessary before even a reasonable degree of success can be assured. If the marks to be obliterated are numerous, the book had better be taken to pieces by removing the cover and separating the leaves, first cutting the binder's threads and taking especial care not to *tear* anything. Each leaf must then be examined, both on the flat and when held up to the light, for it is essential that the particular description of dirt should be identified as closely as possible.

If grease is apparent, it should first of all be removed, as its presence will interfere with some of the subsequent processes. With this object, the leaf must be laid perfectly flat on a sheet of glass and the grease marks damped out with a pad of cotton wool moistened with benzine. Rubbing is never resorted to; the spots must be merely patted over and over again until they disappear, which they will do after a time. Sometimes the text itself will vanish as well, but whether it will do so or not depends upon the character of the paper and the quality of the printer's ink. If there is any danger, benzine should not be used, as the whole sheet may be cleared of grease marks almost equally well by covering it with a layer of chalk, placing a piece of blotting paper on the top of it, and pressing with a hot iron. Each leaf will, if necessary, have to be treated in the same way, and it may occasionally be found necessary to work on both sides of the paper.

When this process is complete, the next step is to give each leaf a good general cleaning, and this may be done effectually by placing it in a leaden trough and pouring upon it a shallow surface of water. Two or three days of exposure to the rays of the sun will bleach the paper perfectly white, and all kinds of stains except fixed dyes will come out. The leaf is then dried (not in the sun or it will turn yellow), and is ready for the next process. It may happen that the sun is not available for this, or, indeed, any other purpose, and when such is the case, the surface dirt may be bleached off with a solution of chloride of lime in the proportion of one part to forty of water. The paper must be soaked in cold water before this mixture is poured on it, and both sides must be operated upon. This solution being essentially weak—if it were otherwise it would eat into the material—it is possible that it may be found unequal to the task of removing some of the more obstinate stains, which must therefore be touched with nitro-hydrochloric acid. Finally, the leaf must be well washed in a stream of running water, and allowed to dry naturally.

Another method of removing surface stains sometimes used by restorers is to cover the paper with a thin layer of fine powdered salt. Lemon juice is then squeezed on the surface in sufficient quantities to dissolve the mineral, and the subject finally washed in boiling water. The chief objection to this process is the use of hot water, which, as may well be imagined, is apt to pulp the paper, or in some cases even to efface the printed text.

Stains which cannot be removed by these processes are of several kinds. Lead pencil marks, for instance, will become fixed if the paper is damped, and they should therefore be helped out first of all with fine bread crumbs. Indian ink stains give way before a camel's hair brush and a cup of hot water, and all kinds of grease marks yield to benzine, turpentine, or ammonia.

Lead stains can be got rid of by an application of peroxide of hydrogen, or even hydrochloric acid; but the greatest care will have to be exercised in handling the latter, or it will corrode the paper in a very short time, causing it to crack and break to pieces. If mixed with its own weight of water, and to three parts of this compound one part of red oxide of lead is added, its power for evil will be very materially diminished; but even under these circumstances it is dangerous to use.

Each of these remedies has to be very carefully undertaken, as the fatty matters in the printer's ink are exceedingly liable to resolve, in which case the book will be spoiled. With care and attention I doubt not that almost any book can be very materially improved, if not made quite as good as new, by a combination of the processes described; and the best plan is to practise on some dirty and worthless specimen until the requisite degree of proficiency is attained.

A "Literary Note" in the magazine entitled *Book Lore* for July, 1887, observes as follows: "The renovation of books is, of course, a work of art in itself, and so clever are experts in the manipulation thereof, that many a dirty and decrepit volume has left their hands looking quite fresh and new. One of the most difficult processes has hitherto been to take dirt off the leaves without injuring the print. With this object bread crumbs were at one time used; but modern science has discovered three ways of effecting the same object in a much more satisfactory manner. Oxalic acid, citric acid, and tartaric acid, when in solution, will eliminate every trace of dirt without in any way acting on the printer's ink. Writing ink is not, however, proof against the attack of any one of the three, and this, too, being considered for the most part as 'dirt,' comes out with the rest. If the leaf is afterwards bleached with chloride of lime, the regenerating process is complete. The remedy for oil stains, it may be observed, is sulphuric ether. If the stains are extensive, it is best to roll up each leaf and insert it into a wide-mouthed bottle half full of ether, shaking it gently up and down for a minute or so. On its removal the oil marks will be found to have disappeared, and, as ether rapidly evaporates, a little cold water is all that is afterwards required. Mineral naphtha and benzoline each possess the property of dissolving oils fixed and volatile, tallow, lard, wax, and other substances of this class."

Worm-holes, another source of disquietude to the collector, are caused by grubs, which are popularly supposed to be the larvæ of beetles. They bore a circular hole through all the leaves, utterly destroying the appearance of any volume upon which they have fixed their attention.

The book worm has a pedigree in comparison with which the family tree of a Howard or a Talbot is a wretched weed. Lucian, in days remote, chides the voracious worm, and other ancient authors have called attention to its ravages. Another pest, called the "acarus," feeds on the paste and glue in the binding; in fact, these two parasites between them will very quickly digest the contents of an ordinary-sized book unless steps are taken for their destruction. The late Sir Thomas Phillipps, in a communication to the British Association in 1837, observes: "My library being much infested with insects, I have for some time turned my attention to the modes of destroying them, in the course of which I observed that the larva of certain kinds of beetles does not seek the paper for food, nor the leather, but the paste. To prevent their attacks, therefore, in future bound books the paste used should be mixed up with a solution of corrosive sublimate, or, indeed, with any other poisonous ingredient. But to catch the perfect insects themselves, I adopt the following plan: *Anobium striatum* commonly deposits its ova in beech wood, and is more partial, apparently, to that than any other wood. I have beech planks cut, and smear them over, in summer, with pure fresh paste (*i.e.*, not containing anything poisonous). I then place them in different parts of the library where they are not likely to be disturbed; the beetles flying about the room in summer time readily discover these pieces of wood, and soon deposit their eggs in them. In winter (chiefly) the larva is produced, and about January, February, and March I discover what pieces of wood contain any larvæ by the sawdust lying under the planks, or where it is thrown up in hillocks on the top of them. All the wood which is attacked is then burnt for firewood: by this simple method I have nearly extirpated *Anobia* from my library."

To surprise and capture a book worm was at one time looked upon as an impossible task; but lately a few successes have been chronicled, but only a few. In order to ward off their insidious attacks, many devices more or less satisfactory have been proposed, but none appear to be absolutely preventative. Dr. Hermann, a noted bibliophile of Strassburg, after careful experiments, has come to the conclusion that a combination of safeguards such as he suggests will have the desired effect of putting to flight not only the worm itself but all other enemies of the library, always excepting biblioklepts and borrowers, against whom there is no defence. The combination suggested by Dr. Hermann certainly seems sufficiently powerful to resist almost any attack, in the same degree that a huge man-of-war may be considered invulnerable when exposed to the assaults of some cockle-shell of a boat. The only objection is the immense amount of trouble and labour involved in preparation, as will readily be perceived after a perusal of the preventives, ten in number.

1. Abolish the use of any wood in the binding processes. 2. Recommend the bookbinder to use glue mixed with alum in place of paste. 3. Brush all worm-eaten wood in the repositories of books with oil or lac varnish. 4. Preserve books bound in calf by brushing over with thin lac varnish. 5. No book to lie flat. 6. Papers, letters, documents, &c., may be preserved in drawers without any danger provided the wafers are cut out and that no paste, &c., is between them. 7. The bookbinder is not to use any woollen cloth, and to wax the thread. 8. Air and dust the books often. 9. Use laths separated one from the other one inch in place of shelves. 10. Brush over the insides of bookcases and the laths with lac varnish.

Dr. Hermann cannot at any rate be charged with any such sentimental regard for "vermin" as that which influenced Mr. Day, a well-known book hunter of the earlier part of the present century. One day, upon removing some books at the chambers of Sir William Jones, a large spider dropped upon the floor, upon which Sir William, with some warmth, said, "Kill that spider, Day! Kill that spider!" "No," said Mr. Day, with that coolness for which he was so conspicuous, "I will not kill that spider, Jones; I do not know that I have a right to do so. Suppose, when you are going in your carriage to Westminster Hall, a superior being, who perhaps may have as much power over you as you have over this insect, should say to his companion, 'Kill that lawyer! Kill that lawyer!' How should you like that? I am sure to most people a lawyer is a more noxious insect than a spider."

The simplest protection yet discovered against book worms is a liberal use of common snuff, which should be sprinkled all over the shelves, the process being repeated every three or four months. This is almost infallible, and probably quite as effectual as Dr. Hermann's ten preventives rolled into one. There is no magic in the art of preserving books—the great art is to be able to get them, and to know what to buy and how much to give for them. This acquired, the rest will come easily enough. The contents of a whole treatise on the custody and preservation of books might be very accurately and succinctly summed up in a few lines. Keep out damp, let the shelves be lined if possible with good leather, and last, but by no means least, look at the insides of your books as well as at the outsides.

Collectors of books are continually being asked to lend volumes which happen to take the passing fancy of a friend or even chance acquaintance, and it is frequently a matter of some delicacy to refuse. Not one person in a hundred knows how to treat a book properly, and the borrower is therefore usually regarded as but one degree removed from an enemy. Curiously enough, the famous bibliophile, Grolier, stamped his books with a motto of invitation, "*Jo Grolierii et Amicorum*". So did Charles de Savigny, who went to even greater lengths still with his legend, "*Non mihi sed aliis*". The private history of neither of these enthusiasts states how they fared, or how many choice tomes were returned dog-eared and stained, even if they were returned at all. For my part I possess no books that I should fear to lend, as my whole library consists of "working copies," useful, probably, but not valuable. The amateur who is the proud owner of a single book out of the common should hide it from the borrower even as from a book worm. He may well lay the couplet which graced the library doors of Pixérécourt to his heart: —

> "*Tel est le triste sort de tout livre prêté
> Souvent il est perdu, toujours il est gâté*".

CHAPTER VII.

THE ALDINE PRESS.

THE revival of classical literature in Europe is generally assigned to the middle of the fifteenth century, and is, perhaps, coeval with the invention of printing, when for the first time it became possible to multiply books not only rapidly but without the multitude of mistakes which invariably occurred in ordinary manuscripts. We have seen that in the palmy days of Rome some of the large publishing houses were quite capable of turning out extensive editions at a few hours' notice. No modern type-setter could possibly keep pace with one of the trained slaves of Atticus, and when some hundreds of the latter were assembled in a room transcribing the MS. of some favourite author through the medium of a professional reader, many copies would be completed in an incredibly short space of time. If, however, the reader made a mistake, it would be faithfully and universally reproduced, while in addition each transcriber might fairly be credited with a number of errors of his own. To this extent the printing press was a great improvement. If it did its work more slowly, less workmen were required; and though each movement of the machine would perpetuate the same errors, these might be reduced to a minimum by the very simple expedient of carefully reading and correcting the "proofs".

The year 1450 ushered in, as is supposed, the great art which was destined to revolutionise the world; and although the pen was employed for many years after that, it gradually gave place to its more convenient if less nimble rival, taking at last a position more congenial to it. "The pen for the brain, the press for reproduction," became henceforth a motto which had for its basis a new division of labour as convenient as it was efficacious.

In the same year,[7] at Sermonetta, a little Italian town, Aldus Manutius, the great printer and editor, first saw the light. The earlier portion of his life was devoted entirely to scholastic duties and in preparing himself, by hard and assiduous study of the Greek and Latin classics, for the more important work of revising and printing the text. It was not until 1490 that the preliminaries were complete, and he found himself, with a little money and an immense stock of knowledge, a comparative stranger at Venice, where already 160 printers and publishers had been engaged for some time in glutting the market with almost worthless books. The old Greek manuscripts especially were a source of inconceivable trouble and

---

[7] M. Firmin-Didot inclines to the year 1449 for the date of Aldus' birth—*vide* his *Alde Manuce et l'Hellenisme à Venise*, p. 1, Paris, 1875.

continual annoyance. They were written for the most part in bastard characters, and crowded with mistakes and omissions, the result of some hundreds of years of repeated transcriptions. They were, moreover, almost as difficult to procure as they were corrupt in text. Nor was this the only difficulty that faced the intrepid pioneer editor. Greek was a language but rarely used, having given place to Latin in all but the most cultivated circles; the demand for books in that character was accordingly limited, while even at that early period competition was ruinous. To say nothing of the army of printers at Venice, there was a large number at Rome who more than supplied the Italian and foreign markets, turning out books in such profusion that the important and oldest printing house, that of Sweinheym & Pannartz, was compelled to petition the Pope to save themselves from bankruptcy. In their petition they state that they had printed no less than 12,475 separate volumes, a statement most likely exaggerated, but none the less cogent evidence of the fierce struggle which was being carried on when Aldus determined to swell the ranks of the already crowded profession.

He was disgusted with the slipshod efforts of the ignorant proprietors of these numerous printing shops, who were so eager to forestall one another that they could not pay any attention to the quality of their work, even assuming they had the aptitude for doing so. He took his stand upon his accomplishments alone, apparently not doubting for an instant that conscientious work, coupled with a superior education, would in the long run repay him for the years of anxious toil which he well knew would be his lot.

The Greek types of Rome, Milan, and Florence, hitherto in use, and all cut to a single pattern, were abominable, and Aldus commenced by casting types of his own. A fount of Roman and Italian letters consisted of only 24 capital and an equal number of small letters—the J and U were the same as I and V—but a complete collection of Greek types with all the varied accents and double characters, with which the language abounds, amounted to no less than 600. Many of these he was compelled at the outstart to forego, and he set to work upon his first book, the *Grammatica Græca* of Lascaris, with barely a tithe of that number. It was well that Aldus should commence with this work, for it was the first which had been printed in Greek, some eighteen years previously by Paravisinus, of Milan, whose small and crabbed type presents a remarkable contrast to that of Manutius. Closely following upon this venture comes the *Editio Princeps* of Aristotle, which, in its 5 vols. folio, is unquestionably the most splendid and lasting monument of the Aldine press. It was issued, one volume at a time, between the years 1495-8, and was sold by the editor and publisher for a sum equivalent to about £5 of our money. Next comes the *Editio Princeps* of Aristophanes, also in folio, and dated 1498, which, like all the other productions of this press at that early date, was printed from large open types with broad margins. The expense of production and consequent cost of these sumptuous volumes were great, too great in fact to command a speedy sale, and Aldus at last began to realise that it was infinitely preferable to print and sell a large number of works at a cheap price than a smaller number at a high one. Accordingly he had a more minute fount of type cast, and in April, 1501, published his famous *Virgil*, a small book of 228 unpaged leaves, measuring not quite 8 inches by 4. The text, so it is said, was modelled after the neat handwriting of Petrarch, and became known throughout Italy as the Aldino type, though in France it was called *Italic*, the name it goes by to this day throughout Europe. This book was sold for about 2s. of our money, and was the first serious attempt ever made to produce cheap printed classics.

No sooner was the success of this venture assured than an unknown printer of Lyons took advantage of the opportunity to issue a wretched reprint, alike in every detail except the quality of the workmanship. Aldus' painstaking textual corrections were slavishly copied: even his title-page was stolen, and the whole immoral production foisted on the public as a genuine example from Venice, and at a little more than half the cost. Horace and Juvenal, Martial and Ovid, shared the same fate as fast as they issued from the legitimate press; the Lyonnese printer was as persevering as he had proved himself unscrupulous, and kept good time with the movements of Aldus. But the fame of the latter was proof against servile imitations, his types alone being so extravagantly praised by his admirers that there were some who seriously contended that their beauty was owing to the silver of which they were made. There is, indeed, no mistaking them, and the collector has only to place an original side by side with one of the reprints from Lyons, to fix the superiority distinctly and irrevocably in his mind. Aldus during his life printed altogether 126 editions known to bibliographers, 78 of which are in quarto or folio, and many in two or more volumes. Some of these consist of choice copies printed on white linen paper, notably the *Opera* of Ovid and Plutarch, and many more passed through several editions during his lifetime and after his death, which, to the great loss of the world of letters, took place on the 6th February, 1515, when he was 65 years of age.

The distinguishing mark of the Aldine press is the well-known dolphin and anchor which first makes its appearance on the edition of the *Terze Rime* of Dante of 1502, and with few exceptions on all the books afterwards issued from the press. The story is that Aldus was engaged in printing Columna's *Hypnerotoma-chia Poliphili*, which appeared in 1499 (a good copy sold in February last for £80), and which contained numerous illustrations, most probably by Andrea Mantegna. One of these represents a dolphin twining about an anchor, a mark so pleasing to Aldus that he subsequently adopted it, using it over his office door as well as on the title-pages of all his books.

At the death of Aldus Manutius his son Paolo, or Paulus, being only three years of age, went to reside with his maternal uncle Andrea Torresano, himself a famous printer of Asola, who subsequently, with his sons, carried on the Aldine press at Venice for the benefit of the parties interested. From that date until 1524 most, if not all, of the books printed at the press bear the imprint: "In ædibus Aldi et Andreæ Asulani soceri," and though, as usual, bearing the anchor, a fresh block had been cut which slightly alters its appearance.

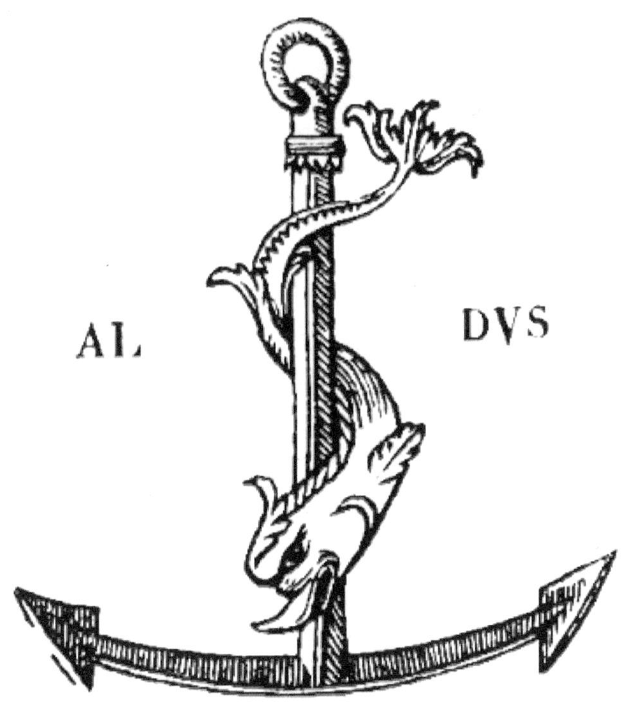

The first Aldine Anchor, 1502-1515.

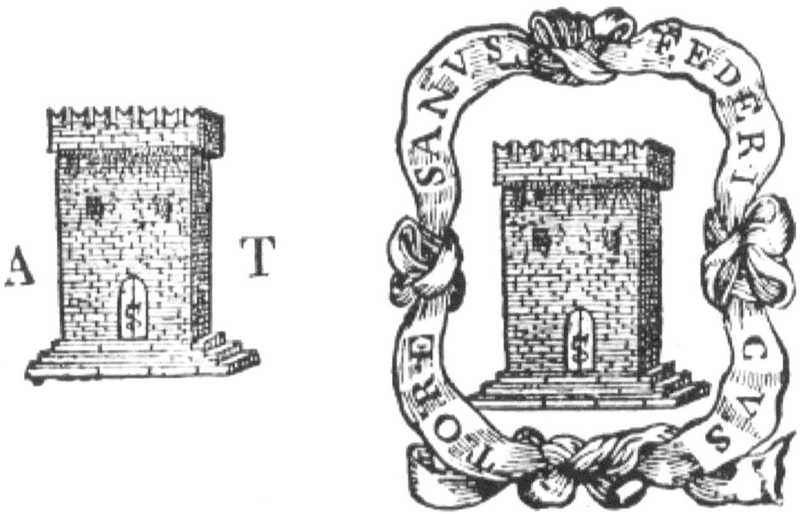

Mark of A. Torresano, and that of his Sons.

The second Aldine Anchor, 1519-1524. Last appearing in this form on the "Homer" of 1524, the first anchor being again used from 1524 to 1540.

From the year 1524 to 1529, when Torresano died, an exact copy of the *first* anchor was again employed and continued to be so used until 1540, when Paulus Manutius, the son of Aldus, took exclusive possession of his father's business. It will be noted that during the three years following the death of Torresano (1530-31-32) no books were issued from the press; and when it recommenced operations in 1533, it was for the benefit of Paulus Manutius and the representatives of Torresano "In ædibus hæredum Aldi Manutii et Andreæ Asulani soceri". In 1540, as before stated, Paulus Manutius took entire control of the business, and a third variation of the anchor was introduced, the inscription on the title-pages being "apud Aldi Filios".

The third Aldine Anchor, 1540-1546, called the Ancora grassa.

The fourth Aldine Anchor, 1546-1554.

From 1546 to 1554 yet another variation of the anchor was adopted, sometimes without the surrounding device. In 1555 a slight modification of the *third* anchor, surrounded sometimes with scroll work, came into fashion again, and so continued until the death of Paulus Manutius on the 6th of April, 1574.

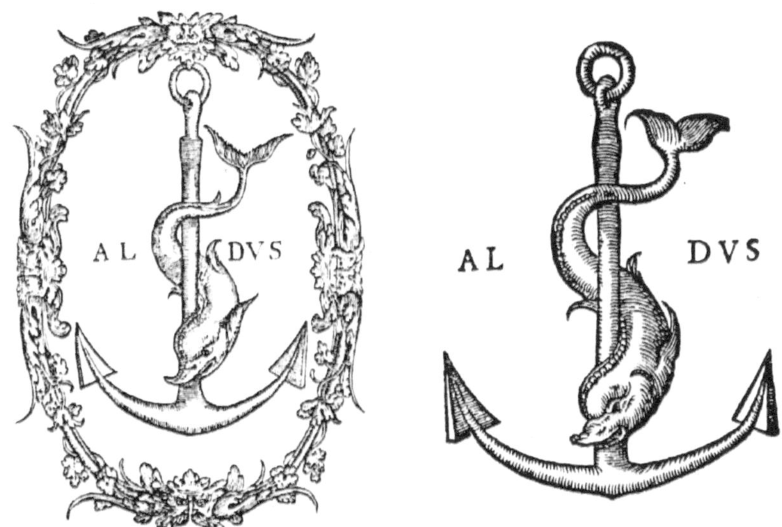

Modification of the third Anchor, 1555-1574.

With the death of Paulus, the glory of the Aldine press departed. He, like his father, had patiently striven to infuse neatness and accuracy into his work, and is said to have been in every respect his equal.

Aldus, the son of Paulus, who is known among bibliographers as "the younger," had not perhaps the same opportunities as were afforded to his predecessors. The art of printing had advanced universally, and there was not so much room for improvement as there had been formerly. He printed in a good, but by no means exceptional, style, from 1574 until the time of his death in 1597, when the Aldine press ceased to exist. During a period of 103 years some 823 books had been issued, many of which are among the prizes of book collecting.[8]

Aldus Junior, like his father and grandfather, used the anchor, but between the years 1575-81 it is so hidden in the foliage of a magnificent coat-of-arms which had been granted to the family by the Emperor Maximilian, that it is likely to be overlooked by any who have not made the Aldine press their special study.

The Aldine Anchor, enclosed in a coat-of-arms, as used by Aldus Junior, 1575-1581. On some occasions, and always after the latter date, he used the anchor alone, sometimes without the word ALDVS.

The collector will need to be cautioned against accepting every work bearing the anchor as a genuine example from the Aldine press. Some are mere forgeries, but so badly executed as to deceive nobody who has seen half-a-dozen of any of the originals. Some printers assumed the mark by licence, as did Torresano, who used Anchor No. 3, with the words "Ex Aldina Bibliotheca," and occasionally Anchor No. 1, but, these exceptions apart, it may usually be taken for granted that a

[8] In addition to this number there are about sixty "Doubtful Editions". The number of recognised Forgeries is about forty-five.

book if well printed and bearing the mark in question is authentic. If any doubt exists it is easy to turn to the pages of Renouard, where every genuine example is catalogued and described. Some fifty years ago, Aldine collectors were more numerous than they are now, and as a consequence prices were higher. This particular branch of bibliography demands the sacrifice of much time, and cannot be even approached without a fair knowledge of Latin, Greek, and French. As a consequence, the new school of collectors, whose knowledge of those languages is not always as well grounded as it might be, have long since severed their allegiance from old traditions and now confine their attention to sober English, where, it must be admitted, there is plenty of scope for good work.

Even yet, however, the earlier productions of the Aldine press maintain their former position: perhaps they have even surpassed it, for as specimens of ancient typography they stand unrivalled. Reference is made chiefly to works dated before 1500, and to such exceptional specimens as the *Virgil* of 1501, some of which are still worth more than their weight in gold. The majority of works from this famous press have, however, fallen enormously in value of late years, as witness the fine copy of Augurellus, 1505, 8vo, beautifully bound in blue morocco, which quite recently was sold by auction for less than a sovereign: some few years ago it would have brought three times the amount, and been considered cheap even then.

By way of illustration, I cannot do better than give a few examples of modern prices, comparing them with the approximate amounts which would have been obtained some twenty-five or thirty years ago.

Homeri Opera, 2 vols. 8vo, red morocco extra, gilt edges, *Venetiis*, Aldus, 1524, £3 15s. Would have sold for £9 or £10.

Silius Italicus de Bello Punico, old Venetian binding, gold tooling, lettered in gold, gilt edges, *Venetiis*, Aldus, 1523, £1 18s. Would have sold for about £5.

Virgilius, cura Aldi Pii Manulii, red morocco, gilt edges, by Roger Payne, *Venetiis*, Aldus, 1514, £4 5s. Sold in 1825 at from £10 to £12 in equally good binding.

Psalterium Græce, a fine copy, in blue morocco, with gilt edges, *Venetiis*, Aldus, no date, but about 1498, £12. Notwithstanding the fact that this is one of the few fifteenth century books from the Aldine press, its value has declined about 25 per cent.

Quintiliani Institutiones, fine copy in russia, gilt edges, *Venetiis*, Aldus, 1521, on title 1522, 14s. Former price about £4.

Aristophanis Comœdiæ, first edition, fine copy in russia, gilt edges, *Venetiis*, Aldus, 1498, a rare book, £4. Former price about £15.

Thucydidis Historia, first edition, and one of the few copies printed on fine paper, old russia, gilt, *Venetiis*, Aldus, 1502, a very scarce book in this condition, £2 14s. Former price from £12 to £15.

The above examples are taken from a single catalogue, and, if occasion demanded, the list could be indefinitely increased. They will, however, be sufficient to show that if the good old days when Eliot's *Indian Bible* of 1661, now worth considerably more than £500, could have been got for thirty shillings or less, are not likely to return, there is yet plenty of opportunity for picking up rare books at a moderate price, and for much less than would at one time have had to be paid for them.

Who knows that the fashion will not change again some day, and that the most coveted of all volumes will not be choice examples from the Aldine press?

The Elzevir Buffalo's Head, from the "Cæsar" of Leyden, 1635.

CHAPTER VIII.

THE ELZEVIR PRESS.

IF Aldine collectors were at one time numerous and enthusiastic, amateurs who affected the Elzevir press, and were never tired of extolling the excellence of the little books which issued therefrom, were more so. Long before the death of the last member of the great printing family, a whole mass of rules, some of them arbitrary, others founded on subtle distinctions, were already regarded as binding on the community of bibliomaniacs which looked upon *L'Aimable Mère de Jésus* as their pole-star, and *Le Pastissier François* as something to be seen only on rare occasions, and to be touched, if touched at all, with bated breath.

There is something harsh, comparatively speaking, about Aldus and his works. He was the taciturn, frugal-living man of letters, who for five years, as he himself confesses, never spent a single peaceful hour save when he was asleep. His very doors were barred with the inscription—

> "Whoever you are, Aldus entreats you to be brief. When you
> have spoken, leave him."

Compared with this grim old editor-printer of a bygone age, the Elzevirs one and all were literary children, playing with their master's text—children who never grew old, and whose many liberties were not only endured, but excused out of consideration for their engaging ways. They were pirates, too, without exception, but they turned you out well. If they mutilated your text, they at any rate supplied you with the best of paper, ornaments and type; from their hands you emerged a well-dressed gentleman, a little ignorant perhaps, but decidedly aristocratic.

A short sketch of the history of the Elzevir family will be found useful for reference:—

The founder of the family, Louis, was born at Louvain in 1540, and, curiously enough, as in the case of Aldus Manutius, did not establish himself at the scene of his future labours until he was forty years old. In 1580 he started as a bookbinder and bookseller at the University city of Leyden, and at first confined his attention entirely to retailing such works as fell into his hands. Three years later, however, he set up a press and printed his first book, the *Drusii Ebraicarum quæstionum ac responsionum*, 8vo, 1583, which, though desirable, is not to be compared, either in intrinsic merit or in value, with some of the latter productions of the press; in fact, what are known as the "good dates" do not commence until the latter portion of the year 1625. Louis died in 1617, and is remarkable only as the founder of a famous family of printers; not one of his 123 different books can be considered important from a collector's point of view; and although a specialist would no doubt endeavour to make his collection as complete as possible, and with that object might be disposed to pay more for these early examples than anyone else might think it worth his while to pay, even he, if well advised, would draw the line at anything like lavish expenditure. Louis left five sons, whom, with a view to further development, it is necessary to bear in mind—Matthieu, Louis, Gilles (Giles), Joost (Justus), and Bonaventure. The last-named son—Bonaventure—commenced business on his own account as a printer in 1608, and on the death of his father in 1617 he took the management of the Elzevir press. In 1626 he took into partnership Abraham, a son of Matthieu, and the newly-constituted firm, which continued to exist until 1652, are entitled to most of the credit which attaches to the name of Elzevir.

Though the Greek and Hebrew works issued by this firm are inferior to those of Aldus and the Estiennes, their small editions of the Latin and French Classics in 12mo, 16mo, and 24mo cannot be surpassed for elegance of design, neatness, clearness, and regularity of type, as well as for the beauty of the paper which they used. Mention may be made especially of the *Novum Testamentum Græcum*, 1624 and 1633; the *Psalterium Davidis*, 1635 and 1653; the *Virgil* of 1636; and the *Comediæ* of Terence, 1635; though the works which gave the press its chief celebrity were the collection of French authors on History and Politics, in 24mo, known as *Petites Republiques*, and the series of Latin, French, and Italian Classics, in small 12mo.

It seems to be an almost universal belief that all the works issued from the Elzevir press are small in bulk, and various terms, more or less foolish, have been invented by careless or incompetent persons to give expression to this idea. One of them, and perhaps the most hideous of them all, is "dumpy twelves". In the first place, works issued from the Elzevir press in 12mo are perfectly symmetrical in shape, and not at all dumpy; and, secondly, many books are in 4to, some even in folio, as, for example, the *Académie de l'Espée*, printed by Bonaventure and Abraham in 1628. The amateur must avoid being misled by the poetical effusions which from time to time make their appearance, and which for the most part are written by persons who know nothing whatever of the subject. To obtain a rhyme for "Elzevir" is difficult, but it has been done at much sacrifice of common-sense.

Jean, the son of Abraham above mentioned, was introduced into the firm in 1647, five years before it came to an end through the death of the two partners in 1652. On this latter event taking place, he entered into partnership with Daniel, the son of Bonaventure, but the firm was not very successful, and was dissolved by mutual consent in 1655. Jean continued to trade on his own account until 1661, when he died, and Daniel joined Louis, the third of that name, and son of the second Louis, who had been printing at Amsterdam since 1638.

From 1655 to 1666 Daniel and Louis printed a series of Latin Classics in various sizes. Louis died in 1670, and Daniel ten years later.

We now come to the closing years of the press, though reference must be made *en passant* to Isaac, another son of Matthieu, who established a press at Leyden in 1616, and continued to print there until 1625. None of his editions, however, attained any fame.

The last representatives of the Elzevir family were Peter, the grandson of Joost, who, during the years 1667-75, printed seven or eight volumes of little consequence, which were published at Utrecht, and Abraham, the grandson of the first Abraham, who, from 1681 to 1712, was University printer at Leyden. As the family pedigree is considerably involved, or, like most other pedigrees, appears to be so at first sight, I give a chart for the convenience of the reader, with the dates during which each member of the family flourished, omitting, however, the names of many other members of the family, who do not enter into the scope of the inquiry, and who were, in fact, not printers at all.

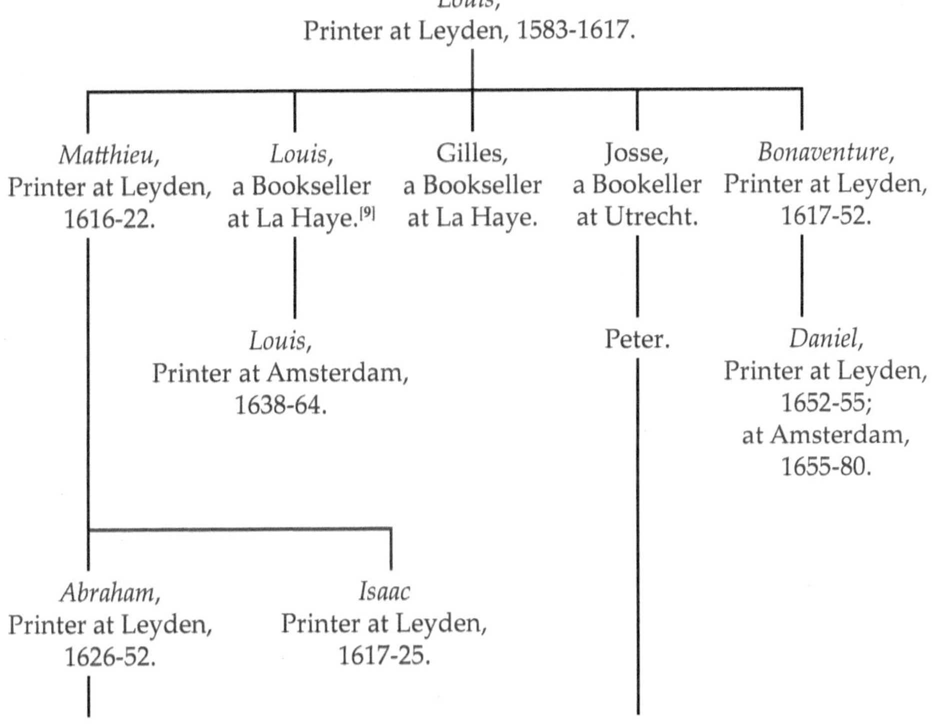

[9] Louis Elzevir II. (1590-1621) produced nine books, one, however, the Navigatio ac Itinerarium of Linschoten, 1599, bearing the name of Gilles Elzevir (probably inserted whilst he was temporarily managing the business of his brother, who in 1599 was called to Leyden to help his father, Louis I.).

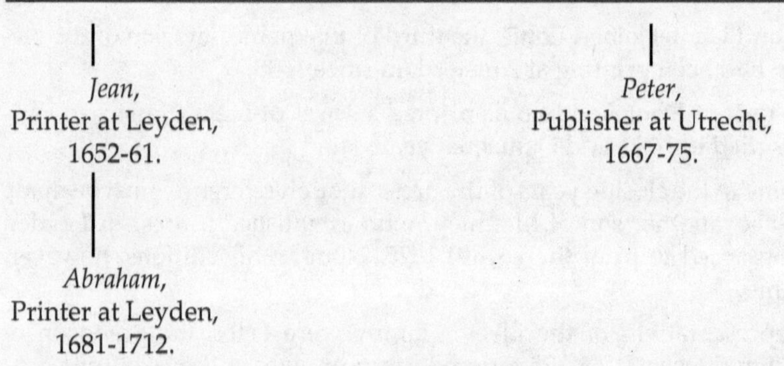

The number of works issued from the press of the Elzevirs, whether at Leyden, Amsterdam, or Utrecht, numbers, according to Willems, 1608 different publications, of which 1213 bear the name or mark of the firm which issued them. Of these latter, 968 are in Latin, 126 in French, and the remainder in Greek, Flemish, German, Italian, and Hebrew. There is also a single volume, printed in English, which seems to have escaped the notice of bibliographers. It is entitled *"Confession of Faith, and the Larger and Shorter Catechisme, &c.,* Amsterdam, printed by Luice Elsever, for Andrew Wilson, and are to be sold at his shop in Edinburgh, 1649". It is usually stated in works of reference that none of the Elzevir publications were printed in English, but the above, if it is genuine, affords an exception.

As every amateur is aware, the Elzevirs frequently—but not always—marked their title-pages with devices, of which the most frequent were the Sphere, the Hermit, Minerva, and the Eagle on a cippus (low column) holding in its claws a sheaf of seven arrows. As each firm adopted or relinquished the family marks to suit its convenience at the time, it becomes necessary to tabulate them for the purpose of avoiding confusion. The number in brackets gives the total number of books, not including catalogues, produced by the firm to which it is annexed.

THE LEYDEN PRESS.

Louis Elzevir. 1583-1617 (102 books).

> Marks.—
> A hand, with the device—"Æqvabilitate".
> An angel with a book.
> The Eagle (with seven darts representing the seven provinces of the Netherlands) on a cippus, with the inscription—"Concordia res parvæ crescunt" (most frequent).
> A book of music, opened.

Matthieu and Bonaventure Elzevir. 1617-1622 (71 books).

> Marks.—
> The Eagle on a cippus.
> The book of music, opened.
> The Hermit, first appearing on the *Acta Synodi Nationalis,* 1620 (Isaac Elzevir), motto—"Non solus".

Of the three marks mentioned above the first and last were more usually employed.

Isaac Elzevir. 1617-1625.

Marks.—   Two hands holding a cornucopia (rare).
             The Eagle on the cippus.
             The Hermit.

Bonaventure and Abraham Elzevir. 1622-1652 (514 books).

Marks.—   The Hermit (most frequent).
             The Eagle on a cippus.
             The Sphere, first appearing on the *Sphæra Johannis de Sacro-Bosco*, 1626.
             The Arms of the University.
             A palm tree with the device "Assvrgo pressa".[10]
             Minerva, with her attributes (the olive tree and the owl) and the motto "Ne extra oleas".

---

[10] This was the mark of Erpenius, whose stock was purchased by the Elzevirs.

Jean and Daniel Elzevir. 1652-1655 (55 books).

> Marks.—The Sphere (frequent).
> The Hermit (frequent).
> The Arms of the University.

Jean Elzevir. 1655-1661 (113 books).

> Marks.—   The Hermit.
> The Sphere.

The Widow and Heirs of Jean Elzevir. 1661-1681 (48 books).

> Marks.—   The Hermit.
> Two Angels holding an open book; motto—
> "Immortalité".

Of the books printed by this firm, some bear the imprint: "A Leide, chez Pierre Didier," and also "Ex Officina Danielis et Abrahami à Gaasbeeck".

Abraham Elzevir. 1681-1712 (24 books).

> Marks.—   The Hermit (most frequent).
> The Arms of the University; motto—"Hæc
> libertatis ergo".

[The total number of books printed by the Leyden firm from 1583 to 1712 (129 years) is thus 938.]

THE HAGUE PRESS.

Louis Elzevir II. 1590-1621 (9 books).
Jacob. 1621-1636 (3 books).

> [A total of 12 books in 31 years.]

THE AMSTERDAM PRESS.

Louis Elzevir III. 1638-1655 (231 books).

> Marks.—   The Sphere.
> Minerva (most frequent).

Louis and Daniel Elzevir. 1655-1664 (150 books).

> Marks.—   The Sphere.
> Minerva (most frequent).

Daniel Elzevir. 1664-1680 (260 books).

> Marks.—   The Sphere.
> Minerva.

The Widow of Daniel Elzevir. 1680-1681 (7 books).

> Marks.—   Minerva.

The Sphere; motto—"Indefessus Agendo".
The Eagle; motto—"Movendo".

[A total of 658 books in 43 years.]

After seven books had been published by the representative of Daniel Elzevir, the business was wound up. The ornamental punches, &c., by Christopher Van Dyck, were sold, and most probably melted down.

THE UTRECHT PRESS
(so called, though it was merely a publishing centre).

Peter Elzevir. 1667-1675 (10 books).

Marks.—   The Sphere.
                The Hermit.
                Minerva sitting under an olive tree; motto—"Pallas Trajectina semper Augusta".

[The total number of books produced by the whole family during 129 years amounts to 1618 works.]

The above are the chief, but by no means the only, marks used by the various members of the family. The few which have not been noticed occur only at rare intervals, and are of but little importance. One device, representing a bees' nest, with a fox and the motto "Quaerendo," though frequently ascribed to the Elzevirs, is in reality none of theirs, being the mark of Abraham Wolfgang, a Dutch printer of considerable repute.

The Elzevirs, as before stated, were pirates, who thought nothing of reproducing the full title-page, with the original publisher's name, and, when this is the case, it is often a matter of very great difficulty to distinguish between the original and the reprint. Again, when these printers did not wish to put their name to any particular work, for fear of embroiling themselves with the Government, they either marked it with the Sphere or else adopted a pseudonym. Thus Jean and Daniel frequently marked their title-pages "A Leyde, chez Jean Sambix," the Amsterdam printers occasionally adopted "Jacques le Jeune," while "Nic Schouter" was a favourite fictitious name. These pseudonyms are, however, much less numerous than was at one time supposed. The first reproduction of the *Provincial Letters*, by Louis and Daniel Elzevir, of Amsterdam, bears on the title-page, "A Cologne, chés Pierre de la Vallée, 1657"; that of 1659, by Jean Elzevir, of Leyden, has "A Cologne, chez Nicolas Schoute". A *Recueil de Diverses Pièces servant à l'Histoire de Henry III.*, &c., bears "A Cologne, chez Pierre du Marteau"; *Les Imaginaires*, of the Sieur de Damvilliers, in its two parts purports to be issued "A Liége, chez Adolphe Beyers". *Il Divortio Celeste*, with other works of Pallavicini, dates from Villafranca, while other undoubted productions of the Elzevir press were ostensibly published "A Mons, chez Gaspard Migeot; Londini, typis Du Guardianis; Stampati in Cosmopoli," and so on, through a list which, difficult enough to remember, is yet not very extensive.

It will be readily seen that the knowledge requisite for a collector to possess, if indeed he wishes to become a master of his subject, is of no mean order, for not only must he have the family pedigree at his fingers' ends, and be capable of detecting a pseudonymous or pirated work, but he must also be in a position to appreciate the "right dates," and to detect an improper head or tail piece when he sees it. Some books which pass as Elzevirs are in reality spurious, even though marked with the "Sphere" or other device; others, though coming from the press, are inferior editions, "not of the right date," as the specialist puts it.

One of the most beautiful little books ever issued from the Elzevir or any other press is the *Cæsar* of 1635, which, on referring to the table, we shall see must have been printed by Bonaventure and Abraham at Leyden.[11] It is in 12mo, and there are no less than three editions, the first and second being so much alike that no one could detect the difference without the most careful of careful inspections. The "right" *Cæsar* is the first, and may be recognised from the Buffalo's Head on a scroll at the head of the dedication. Pages 149, 335, and 475 are misprinted 153, 345, and 375 respectively in the first edition, and there are 35 lines to the page. The second edition, which has not, pecuniarily speaking, a tenth part of the value, has 37 lines to the page, and the misprints are corrected. Another fine work, the *Comediæ* of Terence, Leyden, 1635, 12mo, passed through five editions, all of which are very much alike. The first and "right" edition has, however, on page 51, the word *laches* printed in red, while page 101 is improperly numbered 69. In the second edition *laches* is in black, in the fifth it changes to red again, so that the greatest caution has to be exercised lest the first and fifth editions should be confounded. The former is worth much more than the latter, as the unfortunate purchaser will find to his cost when he comes to sell again.

As previously stated, the "good dates" begin from 1625, the year when Bonaventure and Abraham went into partnership at Leyden, and any books dated from that year to 1655, when Jean and Daniel dissolved partnership, are most likely to be of value, provided only the right edition is forthcoming. Daniel was, however, by far the best printer in the family, though some make an exception in favour of Bonaventure and Abraham; and as he continued in business at Amsterdam, either by himself or in conjunction with Louis from 1655 to 1680, those dates must also be considered "good". From the Amsterdam press, in 1655, issued that prize of Elzevir collectors, the *Pastissier François*, and the splendid *Virgil* of 1676 in *grand* as well as *petit format*, or as we should say in English, on large and small paper. The halcyon days of the press at Leyden date from 1625 to 1655; those of the press at Amsterdam from 1655 to 1680.

It is, of course, impossible for anyone, be he dealer or amateur, to carry in his head all these details and distinguishing marks, and reference in cases of doubt will have to be made to Willem's *Les Elzevier*, a work which has superseded all others on the subject. With this book at hand it is difficult to go wrong, as the minutest points of difference are chronicled with great fidelity.

We will now take it for granted that the amateur is in full possession of, or can obtain, all the information necessary to enable him to distinguish between a right and a wrong date. He has still, however, to bear in mind that even a right-dated volume may be in such a wretched condition as to be hardly worth purchasing. If

[11] The imprint is merely *Lvgdvni Batavorum, ex officina Elzeviriana.*

he will take a walk down Holywell Street he may frequently meet with genuine Elzevirs which the dealers will be only too glad to dispose of for a shilling or two each. The reason of this is that, not only are the works offered for sale *not* "of the good date" (*i.e.*, inferior editions), but they are also, in the vast majority of instances, battered, dirty, and, worse than all, "cropped," sometimes even to the very headlines. For a dirty book there is some hope, since it may be possible to clean it, but for a cropped specimen there is none: like Lucifer, it has fallen from its high estate "never to rise again".

As the measurement of these small books is always made in millimetres, 25·4 of which go to the inch, the enthusiastic collector carries with him an ivory rule on which the French measures are marked. The *Ovid* of 1629, 3 vols. 16mo, runs to 127 millimetres; the *Cæsar* of 1635 to 130 millimetres—anything below 125 millimetres is hardly worth looking at; the *Virgil* of 1676, if uncut, reaches as high as 148 millimetres, or, if in *grand format*, even to 184 millimetres. A book of high measurement, or entirely uncut, may be worth £100 or more, according to its quality; but if cropped below the fashionable height it would not bring as many shillings. A copy of *Le Pastissier François*, 128 millimetres high, was not long ago offered at 1500 francs, or £60; an entirely uncut copy brought 10,000 francs, or £400; and yet between the two there could not have been a greater difference in height than three, or at the most four, millimetres. The truth is that Elzevirs are measured with the same accuracy observable in the weighing of precious stones, and the 25th part of an inch makes a wonderful difference.

That book collectors sometimes go to extreme lengths cannot be doubted by anyone who has spent much time in their company; but the English bibliophiles are not to be compared in this respect with their French brethren. The latter are *the* collectors of Elzevirs, and will frequently spend enormous sums on specimens which from their appearance and real practical utility are worth hardly anything at all. What can be more incorrect than the Leyden *Virgil* of 1636? It is literally crammed with the most shameful errors, so much so that Heyne says it is destitute of the slightest trace of any good quality. Yet the famous Charles Nodier spent nearly all his life searching for a genuine copy of the first edition, which, when obtained, filled a place purposely left vacant for it. Up to that time he had declined to "profane" his shelves with any *Virgil* at all.

Thus much for the Elzevir press, which, like the Aldine, is not regarded with the same favour by collectors as it formerly was. Nevertheless there are many, particularly in France, who yet make a speciality of these little books with "good dates," and it is, therefore, necessary to know something of them. Of one thing the collector may be quite confident: he has here plenty of material for the study of a lifetime, and, what is greatly to the point, ample opportunity of accumulating a representative series of examples of the press. Good Elzevirs, though rare, are not hopelessly so; while bad ones are as plentiful as blackberries. In this respect, at any rate, the Elzevir collector has a great advantage over many of his fellows, whose hunting-grounds are circumscribed, and who frequently would give anything to obtain even a mutilated copy from the press of their favourite printer.

CHAPTER IX.

THE EARLY ENGLISH PRESSES.

IN the short time that intervened between the invention of printing by means of movable type and the end of the fifteenth century some 20,000 different works are known to have been issued from the European press. Many copies of these are doubtless hidden away in old lumber rooms, or in the recesses of imperfectly cat-alogued libraries of obscure and decaying towns. Some have altogether perished, leaving no trace of their ephemeral existence; others are known by name, but have themselves vanished as effectually as if they had never existed. What, for instance, has become of the fifteen books of Ovid's *Metamorphoses* which Caxton, in his pref-ace to the *Golden Legende*, says that he printed? Hitherto no copy has been un-earthed, nor any fragment of a copy. Where is the *Lyfe of Robert Erle of Oxenford* mentioned in the preface to the *Four Sons of Aymon*? What was the great printer doing between the years 1486-8, during which time, so far as can be discovered, he printed nothing? These and many similar questions are important, as raising a very strong probability that the bibliography of Caxton is very far from being com-plete. The same remarks apply more or less to nearly every other fifteenth century printer. There is a field here which has never been fully explored, and which, in all probability, never will be until some Augustus shall arise, and by a wave of his hand throw open the dwellings, the libraries, and even the outhouses of the world to his troop of eager agents. In the meantime, a single discovery of a hitherto un-known book of the fifteenth century acquires an importance proportionate to the exceptional nature of the occurrence; and though the book hunter never despairs, he knows only too well that such rarities fall only to fortunate mortals like the French bibliophile Resbecq, whose extraordinary luck was proverbial, or to those whose ignorance is so dense that they seem provided, as compensation, with more than a fair share of attractive power. It seems a pity that the unappreciative should often obtain chances which are denied to those who could utilise them to advan-tage, but it is often the case. The merest tyro sometimes experiences a success which the experienced bibliophile sighs for in vain.

Glowing as this picture appears, the collector must not run away with the idea that all early printed books are valuable. Some, even of the fifteenth century, are not worth an Englishman's ransom by a long way. The question of value depends mainly on the name of, and the degree of reputation acquired by, the printer. Thus, books printed by Fust and Schœffer, Gutenberg and Fust, Sweynham and Pannar-tz, and many others of the oldest continental printers, are scarce and valuable in the extreme; so are any books from the presses of the early English printers. On the other hand, the Estienne, Giunta, and Plantin presses are comparatively neglected. Here, again, it is a question of reputation, only, in this case, the inquiry is directed not to the book itself, but to the printer, a reversal of the usual rule, and one that is productive of an extraordinary result, namely, that trivial books are often the most valuable, simply because they have not been worth keeping. Let no one, then, look, in the first instance, to the character of an early printed book, but let him rather study that of the craftsman, keeping in mind the current of popular favour and the direction in which it flows. If he does this, he will find that, so far as this country is concerned, there is a scope amply sufficient to satisfy the most earnest aspirations. The long line of printers from Caxton, in 1477, to Day, in 1546, and, in a lesser degree, those of the subsequent fifty years, discloses names which are graven on the heart of the collector, who often accounts himself fortunate if he can procure a single specimen from the early English press. As the chance of his doing so, though remote, is by no means impossible, seeing that copies are frequently offered for sale while many others must be hidden away, it is necessary that he should have some ideas of his own. To let slip a chance which fortune throws in his way, and which may never occur again, would be productive of never-ending regret, especially as, with a little care and attention, there is no reason why such a disaster should occur.

The subject of the early English press could not, of course, be entered upon fully without occupying considerable space, and I must content myself with such a *résumé* as can conveniently be compressed within the compass of a few pages.

It is worthy of note that many of these old English printers were, like Aldus Manutius, editors as well. In the early days labour was not divided as it is now, and it is well known that Caxton, for example, not merely translated many of his publications, but cast his own type and bound the sheets when ready for publication. Each of these processes was perfected in his own office, and so well that to this day his handiwork is seldom surpassed. Improved apparatus cannot always hold its own against manual dexterity—an observation which becomes more than ever accentuated when we apply it to the art of Typography, perfect in its results almost from infancy.

WILLIAM CAXTON, 1474(?).

Caxton, as, indeed, many of the other printers whose names are subsequently mentioned, used several devices, of which, I think, it will be sufficient to give the chief. This pioneer English printer learned his art during the years 1474-5 in the office of Colard Mansion at Bruges. Sometime about the year 1477 he established himself as a printer at Westminster, where he died in 1491. There are certain distinguishing features by which any of Caxton's works may be known, even if the colophon is lost or the book a mere fragment. His type is *always* Gothic or old English; he never used catchwords nor commas; and although works from the press of Lettou and Machlinia of London (1480) are exactly like Caxton's in these respects, the measurement of any given space occupied by 20 or 22 lines, according to the description of type used, varies considerably. Since 1819, some twenty hitherto unknown works by Caxton have been identified by the measurement test, for a full explanation of which the collector is referred to Blades' *Life of Caxton*.

Among the works printed by this great master may be mentioned the following, which have brought the prices affixed at auction, within the last few years:—

The Game and Playe of Chesse, small folio, 31st March, 1474, the first book of Caxton with a date, and a perfect copy, but wanting the two blank leaves (10⅛ in. × 7⅛; in.), old calf, £645.

Dictes and Sayinges of the Philosophers (11½ in. × 8 in.), 1477, folio, morocco extra, perfect, £650.

Higden's Discripcion of Britayne, evidently made up from two imperfect copies (11½ in. × 8 in.), morocco extra, 1480, folio, £195.

Chronicles of Englonde, 1480, folio, wanted part of the index and otherwise greatly imperfect, £67; another copy (9½ in × 7 in.), perfect, £470.

Higden's Polychronicon, 1482, 4to, a very imperfect copy, containing only 205 leaves, £31.

Ryal Book, or Book for a King, perfect, but several leaves mended (11⅛; in. × 8⅛; in.), no date (1487?), folio, £365.

The Prouffitable Boke for Mannes Soule, called The Chastysing of Goddes Children, no date, folio, quite complete; and another called *The Tretyse of the Love of Jhesu Christ by Wynkyn de Worde*, 1493, folio, both in one volume, £305.

Bœcius de Consolacione Philosophie, in Latin and English, a complete copy, several leaves stained (10¾ in. × 7½ in.), old calf, no date, folio, £156.

Contemporary with Caxton were the printers Lettou and Machlinia, previously mentioned, who carried on business in the city of London, where they established a press in 1480. Machlinia had previously worked under Caxton. Their productions are scarce, but not so much so as those of Caxton. An inferior copy of their *Vieux Abrigement des Statutes*, no date, but about 1481, folio, sold by auction in August, 1887, for £8 10s., and occasionally other and better specimens may be picked up for two or three times that amount.

WYNKYN DE WORDE, 1491.

In all probability this famous printer was one of Caxton's assistants or workmen, when the latter was living at Bruges, but without doubt he was employed in his office at Westminster until 1491, when he commenced business on his own account, having in his possession a considerable quantity of Caxton's type. Wynkyn de Worde, who was one of the founders of the Stationers' Company, died in 1534, after having printed no less than 410 books known to bibliographers, the earliest of which bearing a date is the *Liber Festivalis*, 4to, 1493. The whole of these works, especially when in good condition, are excessively scarce, and invariably bring high prices. A wormed copy of the *Descrypcion of Englonde, Wales, and Scotlonde* brought £10 at the Gibson Craig sale in July, 1887, and the *Vitas Patrum*, 1495, folio, £71, at the Crawford sale in the same month. Voragine's *Golden Legend*, printed by de Worde in 1527, brought £81 a short time ago; his *Higden's Polychronicon*, 1495, folio, wanting title, £16 5s.; the *Nova Legenda Anglie*, 1516, folio (wormed), £28; and Dame Juliana Berner's *Fysyhing with an Angle*, 1496, folio (frontispiece inlaid), £120.

RICHARD PYNSON, 1493.

This early English printer was by birth a Norman, but became naturalised in England by letters patent and was appointed king's printer. He was the first to introduce the Roman letter into this country, though this honour is by some attributed to Wynkyn de Worde. The Italian penmen of the fifteenth century furnished the model for the round character which has been successively adopted in most of the typographical foundries since the days of Pynson, and which is known as the Roman character; and these penmen are supposed to have imitated the writing of the Carlovingian MSS. Thus the small alphabet used by our printers is a copy of that adopted in the churches of France in the time of Charlemagne.

Among Pynson's works may be mentioned the following. The prices affixed have, as before, been realised at auction within the last few years.

Sebastian Brant's *Shyp of Folys of the Worlde*, translated by Barclay, black letter, woodcuts, morocco extra, imperfect, 1509, folio, £23.

Jeronimi de Sancto Marcho Opusculum, &c., woodcut signs of the Zodiac and Pynson's device on title, a fine copy in morocco extra, bound by Bedford (1509), 4to, £85.

Intrationum Liber, woodcut of royal arms, perfect, old russia, 1510, folio, £36 15s.

JULIAN NOTARY, 1498.

The periods of the birth and death of this ancient typographical artist are entirely unknown. One of his books, the *Missale Secundum vsvm Sarvm*, dates from Westminster, the 20th December, 1498, and one or two others are dated 1520, so that it is safe to say that he flourished between those dates. One of the most extraordinary books issued at this early time is the *Shepherd's Calendar*, printed by Julian Notary. It is full of quaint woodcuts, illustrative of religious myths, which, considering the times, are excellently executed. An edition of this calendar was also printed and published by Richard Pynson. The total number of books known to have been printed by Julian Notary is 23.

WILLIAM FAQUES, 1499.

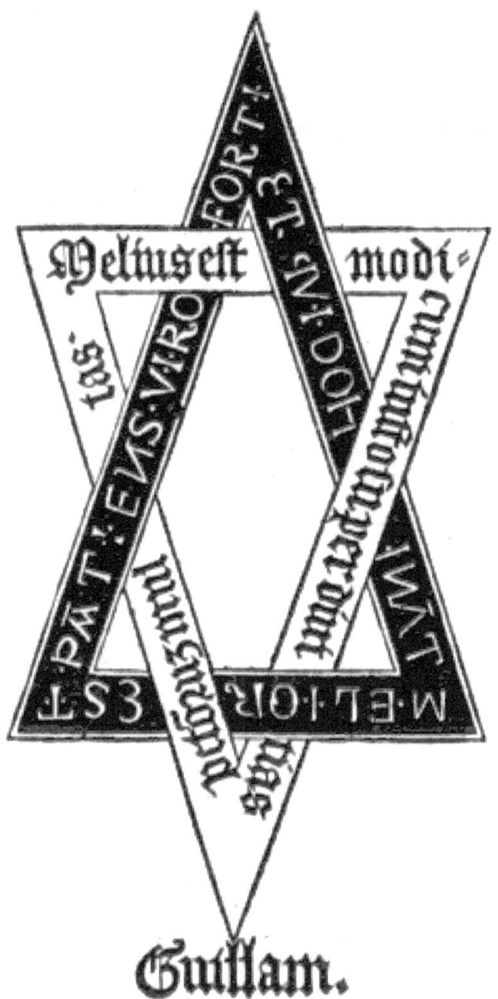

This printer is known in connection with a few books, about half-a-dozen in number, which, as usual, are excessively scarce and very valuable. The dates of his birth and death are uncertain. The first of his books, however, is dated 1499, and the last 1508.

RICHARD FAWKES, 1509.

Although the date of the first book printed by Richard Fawkes is given as 1509, it is more than likely that the date on the title-page (*Salus Corporis, Salus Anime*, folio, 1509) is a misprint. The next in point of date is a book of *Hours*, 1521, and it is hardly likely that twelve years should have elapsed without his printing anything. Still, time has spared such a few of this printer's publications that it is quite possible the date may be correct. Specimens from Fawkes' press are excessively rare, none having been offered for sale, so far as I am aware, for many years.

PETER TREVERIS, 1514.

Our information about this printer is very meagre, so much so that little seems to be known of him beyond the fact that he was the first printer in the borough of Southwark. He printed for John Reynes, a bookseller in St. Paul's Churchyard in 1527; also for Laurence Andrewe, who carried on business in Fleet Street about the same date. Anthony à Wood, in his *History and Antiquities of Oxford*, says that Treveris printed some of Whitinton's pieces there in 1527, but no evidence of the fact appears to be forthcoming. The first book known to have issued from his press is the *Disticha Moralia*, 4to, 1514, though some bibliographers deny that Treveris was the printer. The whole number of his productions, inclusive of the grammatical treatises of Whitinton, which, on the authority of Wood and for purposes of convenience, are ascribed to him, does not amount to 30. They are, as usual, very scarce.

The Grete herball whiche gyueth parfyt Knowledge, &c., black letter, woodcuts, badly cut down, 1529, folio, £5.

ROBERT COPLAND, 1515.

This printer was one of the assistants of Wynkyn de Worde, and a legatee under his will. He was also a stationer and bookseller, dwelling at the Rose Garland in Fleet Street, where he carried on business from about 1515 to the year 1547 or beginning of 1548. His productions are not only few in number, but very rarely ever met with. He seems to have been fond of small and fugitive pieces, of which, doubtless, a large number have perished owing to the popularity which formerly attended publications of this kind. The number of his works catalogued by Ames amounts to 12. This printer must not be confounded with William Copland (*post*), whose productions are, comparatively speaking, common.

JOHN RASTELL, 1520.

According to Bale, this printer was a citizen of London, and married the sister of Sir Thomas More. The date of his birth is not known, but he died in 1536, leaving two sons, one of whom, William, succeeded to his business. Ames mentions 31 works printed by John Rastell and 15 by William, and among the former is the famous *Pastyme of People, or Cronycles of Englond*, of which only three perfect copies are known to exist. A fac-simile reprint was issued in 1811 by Dr. Dibdin. An original copy of this work, which contains 18 woodcut full-length portraits of the kings, was, though imperfect, sold at the Wimpole sale, in June, 1888, for as much as £79. A copy of the reprint is worth about 30s.

JOHN SKOT, 1521.

Books printed by this workman, which are only 13 in number, are seldom seen. Much—and probably it is no exaggeration to say, most—of the work of the English printers of the fifteenth and sixteenth centuries has been destroyed, and it is probable that between the years 1521 and 1537, when John Skot, or Scott, as he sometimes spelled his name, is known to have been working, a large number of publications was issued from his press, of which not a trace remains. There is a good copy of the diminutive tract known as *The Rosary*, printed by Skot in 1537, in the library of Earl Spencer at Althorpe.

ROBERT REDMAN, 1523.

Robert Redman set up a printing press at the house quitted by Pynson, just outside Temple Bar, and called the George. He seems also to have adopted a colourable imitation of his device, and altogether to have taken great advantage of his opportunities to undermine the business of his rival. In the 1525 edition of *Lyttleton's Tenures*, printed by Pynson, the latter takes Redman roundly to task, and in an edition of *Magna Charter*, dated 1527, a similar strain of abuse is maintained. The first book known to have been printed by Redman bears date 1523. He died somewhere about the year 1540.

Fitzherbert's *Diuersite de Courtes*, black letter, 24 ff., 1528, 16mo, £2 10s.

ROBERT WYER, 1527.

This prolific printer was in business, "in the felde besyde Charynge Crosse," from 1527 to about 1542, but as the greater number of his books were published without dates, it is possible that he may have lived beyond the year given. The number of his books catalogued amounts to 68, and they consist chiefly of treatises on Astrology, Medicine, and, more rarely, Poetry.

THOMAS BERTHELET, 1530.

Towards the middle of the sixteenth century the popular demand for biblical legends and treatises on scholastic divinity began to decline, and a taste for classical literature to take its place. The productions of Berthelet, which give evidence of the improvement in this respect to no slight degree, are intrinsically valuable, as well as unusually numerous. Berthelet died about Christmas, 1555, as appears by an entry in the Stationers' Hall books for 26th of January, 1555-6. The number of his works, as catalogued, amounts to 190.

The Praise of Folie, by Erasmus, translated by Chaloner, black letter, wormed, and title mended, 1549, 4to, £2 8s.

Gower's *De Confessione Amantis*, black letter, Berthelet's first edition, wormed, oak boards, covered in stamped leather, 1532, folio, £8.

Institution of a Christen Man, black letter, woodcut border to title by Holbein, morocco extra, 1537, 4to, £22 10s.

Necessary Doctrine and Erudition for any Christen man, black letter, morocco extra, 1543, 4to, £12.

Psalms or Prayers, black letter, wanting title and signature Lv, calf, no date (1548), 8vo, £10 5s.

Henrici VIII. Pia et Catholica Christiani Hominis Institutio, morocco extra, by Pratt, fine copy, 1544, 4to, £5 5s.

JOHN BYDDELL, 1533.

John Byddell first carried on business at the sign of "Our Lady of Pity," and seems to have borrowed his device from one of the earlier pages of Corio's *History of Milan*, 1505. Subsequently he removed to the "Sun," in Fleet Street, formerly occupied by Wynkyn de Worde. This printer died somewhere about 1544, having published 29 volumes, according to Ames, most of which are of a serious character.

Prymer in Englishe, with Calendar and Almanake (1535-54), black letter, title in fac-simile, russia extra, 16th June, 1535, 4to, £97.

Bible in English (by R. Tavener), black letter, several leaves mended, morocco extra, by Bedford, folio, 1539, £57.

RICHARD GRAFTON, 1537.

Richard Grafton, the king's printer, was at one time a citizen and grocer of London, and seems to have been brought up as a merchant. He commenced business as a printer with Edward Whitchurche in or about the year 1537, and from that date to 1541 they continually printed in partnership. The dissolution was probably due to the persecution to which they were subjected on account of the Act of the Six Articles. Whitchurche, whose device is given below, is said to have married the widow of Archbishop Cranmer, and is known to have been living in 1560. Grafton, who was continually in difficulties, and on one occasion narrowly escaped with his life, is supposed to have died about the year 1572.

Boke of Common Praier, black letter, blue morocco extra, by Rivière, August, 1552, folio, £60.

Primer in Englishe (black letter) *and Latyn* (roman type), brown morocco extra, by Bedford, 1545, 4to, £28.

Orarium seu Libellus Precationum, woodcuts, blue morocco, 16mo, 1546, £20 10s.

Marbeck's *Concordance of the Bible*, black letter, title inlaid, russia, small folio, 1550, £1 6s.

Halle's *Chronicle*, black letter, russia extra, by Bedford, folio, 1550, £9.

Harding's *Chronicle*, black letter, morocco extra, by Bedford, 1543, 4to, £11 5s.

The Order of the Communion, black letter, wanted title, morocco, 8th March, 1548, sm. 4to (the only copy known), £55.

EDWARD WHITCHURCHE, 1537.

Byble in Englyshe (Cranmer's), black letter, cut down at the top, morocco extra, by Bedford, folio, 1541, £50.

Booke of Common Prayer, black letter, first edition of Edward VI.'s
Prayer Book, with the rare order for the price, a fine copy in blue
morocco extra, folio, 1549, £155.

Boke of Common Prayer, second edition of Edward VI.'s Prayer Book, a
fine copy in blue morocco, folio, 1552, £100.

Book of Prayers used in the Queen's (Catherine Parr's) *House*, black letter,
a fragment of an unknown edition, 32mo, 1550, £2.

Grafton and Whitchurche, in conjunction, printed the first issue of the *Great* or
Cromwell's Bible, a folio book dated 1539, a fair copy of which was sold at the Crawford sale for £111; also the *New Testament, both in Latin and English, after the vulgare
texte* (Coverdale's version), 1538-39, 8vo, partly printed at Paris by Regnault and
completed in London. Nearly the entire impression was seized and burnt by order of the Inquisition, and the few copies that remain are extraordinarily rare and
valuable.

JOHN WAYLANDE, 1537.

A printer who, according to the best authorities, lived at the sign of the "Blue Garland in Fleet Street," and, in the year 1541, at the sign of the "Sun, against the Conduit". He was in business in 1558.

The Primer in English and Latin, after Salisburye Use, some leaves in fac-simile, bound by Rivière in morocco, 22nd August, 1558, 12mo, £20.

Tragedies of all such Princes as fell from their estates throughe the Mutabilitie of Fortune, translated into Englysh by John Lidgate, black letter, some leaves mended, no date, folio, £4 10s.

Prymer in Latin and Englishe...and Almanacke (1555-71), black letter, brown morocco extra, by Rivière, 1555, sm. 4to, £27.

Prymer in Englishe (black letter) *and Latine* (roman type), *after Salisbury Use, with Calendar, &c.,* woodcuts, calf, 1557, 16mo (only six copies are known), £13.

Prymer in Englyshe, with Calendar, black letter, title in fac-simile, brown morocco extra, *Ihon Mayler for Ihon Waylande,* 1539, sm. 4to (only four copies are known), £91.

WILLIAM MYDDYLTON, 1541.

William Myddylton, or Middleton, succeeded to the business of Robert Redman, which he carried on at the sign of the "George, next to St. Dunstan's Church, in Fleet Street". This printer turned out some 30 different publications, known to bibliographers. There is no doubt, however, that many more must be lost, or remain undiscovered. Myddylton probably died somewhere about the year 1550. Another printer, by name Henry Middleton, flourished about the year 1579. His works are scarce, but not nearly so valuable as those of William.

> Froissart's *Cronycles of Englande, &c.*, translated by Bourchier, 2 vols.,
> black letter, 1525, folio, russia extra, (printed by Myddylton and
> Pinson), £9 12s.

REYNOLD WOLFE, 1542.

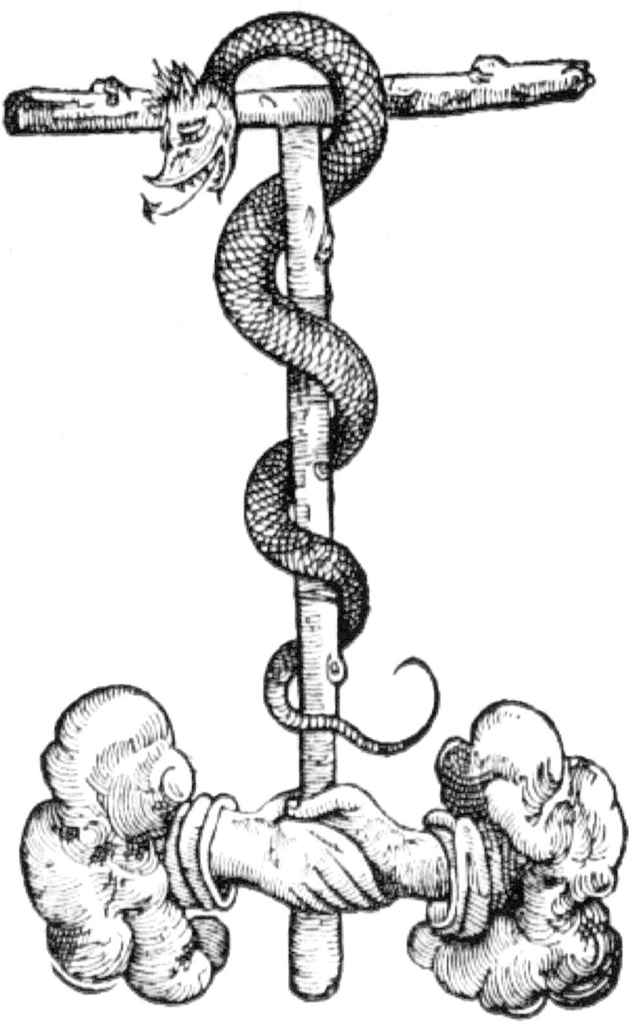

The king's printer, was in all probability a foreigner by extraction, if not by birth. He commenced printing in 1542, but a great portion of his time was spent in collecting materials for an *Universal Cosmography of all Nations*, which, though undigested at his death in 1573, laid the foundation for Holinshed's *Chronicles*. His works are described as being 59 in number, and, as is always the case where any specimens from the presses of early English printers are concerned, are scarce and valuable. After the death of Reynold, his widow, Joan, printed three books, which bear her name. The last of these is dated in 1580, about which time, doubtless, the press ceased to exist.

Care must be taken that this printer is not confounded with others of the same name, who, for the most part, carried on business in France and Holland.

JOHN DAY, 1546.

Next to Caxton and Wynkyn de Worde, this printer certainly ranks the highest in the opinion of bibliographers. Herbert says that Day first began printing a little above Holborn Conduit, and about 1549 removed to Aldersgate. He kept also at the same time several shops in different parts of the town, where his books were sold. Day was the first printer who used Saxon characters, and brought those of the Greek and Italic to perfection. He died in 1584 after having followed the business of a printer for nearly forty years.

The name of John Day will sometimes be found in conjunction with that of William Seres, but rarely, if ever, after 1550. This William Seres was a printer, who, on dissolving partnership with Day in 1550, carried on business by himself for some twenty or twenty-five years in London.

A Short Catechism, black letter, morocco extra, 1553, 16mo, £12.

Booke of Christian Prayers Collected out of the Ancient Writers, black letter, blue morocco extra, by Pratt, 1578, 4to, £26 10s.

Certaine Select Prayers Gathered out of S. Augustine's Meditations, 2 vols., 1575, sm. 8vo, £5 15s.

Psalmes in Metre with Music, black letter, 1571, sm. 4to, £140. This work was sold with another by Jugge and Cawood, and was bound in an exceptionally fine Elizabethan style.

Preces Privatæ in Studiosorum, first ed., 1564, 16mo, also another edition of 1573, 16mo, in two volumes (both printed by William Seres), £3.

WILLIAM COPLAND, 1548.

Probably a son of Robert Copland, though the relationship is very doubtful. It has been supposed that William was a younger brother of Robert, and worked in the office of the latter up to the time of his death, in the same manner as Robert worked in the office of Wynkyn de Worde. It is evident that both William and Robert used the same battered types, which they set up with an equal amount of carelessness. Notwithstanding the workmanship, however, these books are valuable, and always command high prices. The first book of William Copland's printing found with a date is the *Understandinge of the Lorde's Supper*, 1548, 8vo; and between that year and 1568, the time of his death, he is credited with over 60 different publications.

Story of the most noble and worthy Kynge Arthur, black letter, woodcuts, the title and several leaves in fac-simile, morocco extra, 1557, sm. folio, £10; another copy, quite perfect, £30.

The right plesaunt and goodly Historie of the foure sonnes of Aimon, black letter, woodcuts, the title and several leaves in fac-simile, no date or name, but printed by W. Copland in 1554, small folio, £14.

Hystorie of the two Valyaunte Brethren, Valentyne and Orson, black letter, woodcuts, a defective copy, several leaves having been repaired, no date, small 4to, £21.

Among the other old English printers, whose names frequently appear on the title-pages of books, may be mentioned:—

WALTER LYNNE, 1548-50, whose *Cattechismus*, in small 8vo, 1548, brought £59 in June, 1889.

RICHARD JUGGE, 1548-77, *The Holie Bible*, Bishops' Version, black letter, 1568, folio, £70.

THOMAS MARSHE, 1549-87, *Certaine Tragicall Discourses*, black letter, 1567, 4to, £15; also *Heywoode's Woorkes*, 1576-77, 4to, £9 9s.

JOHN CAWOOD, 1550-72, who printed the first collected edition of *Sir Thomas More's Works*, 1557, now worth from £15 to £20, the *Stultifera Navis* of Brant, black letter, woodcuts, folio, 1570, £12, and many others.

RICHARD TOTTEL, 1553-94.

HUGH SINGLETON, 1553-88, *The Supplication of Doctour Barnes*, &c., black letter, morocco extra, by Rivière, no date, 8vo, £10.

JOHN KYNGSTON, 1553-84, the printer of the best folio edition of *Fabian's Chronicle*, 1559.

ROWLAND HALL, 1559-63.

JOHN ALLDE, 1561-96.

ROBERT REDBORNE (cir. 1576), whose only known work is entitled *The history of the moost noble and valyaunt knyght, Arthur, of lytell brytayne*, folio, no date, but about 1576. Of this work only two perfect copies are known. One sold at the Crawford sale in June, 1889, for £27 10s.

THOMAS EST (*cir.* 1592), *Whole Booke of Psalmes*, 1592, 8vo, £15 10s. Wilbye's *Second Set of Madrigales*, half morocco, 1609, 4to, £6. Yonge's Musica Transalpina, 1588, 4to, £7. Yonge's *Musica Transalpina*, the seconde booke, half morocco, 1597, 4to, £11.

With the advent of the seventeenth century presses became very numerous all over England. Christopher and Robert Barker at London, and John Field at Cambridge, are perhaps the best known printers of that era, but the importance and value of their works depend upon circumstances, and cease to exist as a matter of course. It is indeed from this point that the study of English bibliography becomes more difficult and confusing, and here precisely that the young collector is apt to go astray.

The most famous English printer of modern times was undoubtedly John Baskerville; in fact, he seems to have been the only one possessed of exceptional merit. Everyone has heard of Baskerville: he rises the one solitary genius out of the multitude of labourers in the same field, and towers so high above the rest as to eclipse them entirely. Baskerville started as a printer in Birmingham in 1756, having spent hundreds of pounds in the experimental casting of type, which he ultimately brought to the highest state of perfection. Every book printed by him is a masterpiece: his paper is clear and elegant and of a very fine quality, while the uniformity of colour throughout testifies to the care taken in printing every sheet. At one time works from the Birmingham press, presided over by Baskerville, were much sought after, but of late years the fashion has changed and prices have consequently much diminished. The splendid edition of Addison's works, 4 vols., 4to, with portraits and plates, 1761, a beautiful copy bound by Derome in red morocco, brought £10 a short time ago, a depreciation of at least a third in the value, while in some other instances the fall is much more marked. Baskerville appears at one time to have studied the workmanship of the Elzevirs, and on one or two of his books, notably the *Elegantiæ Latini Sermonis* of Meursius, 1757, he has dated the title-page as from *Lugd. Bat. Typis Elzevirianis*. This little volume is a fit tribute to a family of famous printers of the seventeenth century, from a no less excellent workman of the eighteenth, and I feel certain that some day collectors will again vie with each other in collecting choice examples from his press.

CHAPTER X.

BOOKS cannot live long without being bound, and the more expensive and artistic the appearance of the binding, the greater the chance of preservation for the whole. A book is sometimes handled gently, not because of any merits of its own, but simply on account of its cover, which thus becomes its protector in a double sense. Like those old earthen boxes, which on being broken are found to contain the clay tablets of Assyria, many of which run as far back as 1500 years before the Christian era, bindings were doubtless originally intended to act the part of preservatives; beauty of design and even neatness would be after-considerations, and entirely subservient to the sole object, that of protection. By degrees the book lover made demands upon art, and, in obedience to an universal law, the supply answered to his call. Cicero, we are told, was a connoisseur of bindings, and himself employed famous workmen to glorify his rolls of papyrus and vellum, or to bind up his diptychs in the manner of our modern books, but more expensively, if the tastes of the old Roman are not belied, than the majority of book lovers can afford to do in these latter days.

In the palmy days of Rome, art in all its varied forms was probably as advanced as it is now, and we cannot doubt that Virgil and Homer, the representative poets of Rome and Greece, were to be found in a score of palaces, dressed as befitted their high reputation, in the most noble and expensive of coverings. Two thousand years have, however, made a clean sweep of Roman artist and Roman bookman alike, and we have nothing to guide us beyond the casual remarks of one or two diarists and historians of the day, whose chronicles have happened, almost by chance, to come down to us. The names of none of the ancient binders survive, and not a trace of their workmanship remains; we know only that there were such beings, who occasionally threw into their work great taste and skill, and that bibliophiles vied with each other in gaining possession of their choicest examples.

When, therefore, the question is asked, Who was the first binder known to fame? we cannot look to Greece or to Rome for an answer, nor yet to Italy. Curiously enough it is to Ireland that we must turn, for there the monk Dagæus practised the art so long ago as 520 A.D. One example only of his handiwork has survived to our own day, and is now to be found in the library of the British Museum along with the *Textus Sanctus Cuthberti* bound by the first English workman, one Bilfred, a monk of Durham, who flourished nearly 1200 years ago. This *Textus*, so the old legend says, was once swallowed up by the sea, which, respectful of the merits of the saint, gracefully retired fully three miles of its own accord, and so restored the cherished volume to its owners. As the monks were the sole multipliers of books, so also they were, until the invention of printing in 1450, the only binders. Manuscripts of the ninth century are extant, heavily encased in ivory-carved covers or confined between gold and silver plates studded with precious stones. More often than not these expensive coverings were destined to be their ruin, for, to say nothing of private peculation, the sumptuous bindings were ripped off at the time of the Reformation for the sake of the metal or stones, and the manuscripts thrown in thousands upon the tender mercies of the vandals into whose hands they fell.

In the fourteenth century Petrarch was knocked down by one of his own tomes, and was within an ace of breaking his leg, but this was at a period when monastic bindings ordinarily consisted of wood, covered with leather and protected by metallic bosses, corner plates, and massive clasps of iron. Bulk and weight were then the great desiderata, though every now and then the richest materials were still employed in binding, as when a king's library was added to, or some rich monastery gave orders for a sacred volume to be covered with the enamels of Limoges, ivory, gold or silver, and encrusted with jewels.

From the end of the fifth to the middle of the fifteenth century, books were excessively rare and costly, and comparatively few bindings illustrative of the art during the dark ages have been preserved. The few that have survived are wonderful specimens of art, and in every way worthy of the illuminated manuscripts they enclose.

The period of the Renaissance, which is usually assigned to the Pontificate of Leo X., was witness of another change. The ponderous tomes, whose weight was alone a protection, gradually gave way to smaller-sized volumes, and these were often bound in velvet or silk, beautifully embroidered by lady amateurs, perhaps also by professed binders. At other times the monastic covering of wood and leather is observable, and often the leather gave way to seal and shark skin without any tooling or other ornamentation.

These different styles of binding continued in vogue side by side until the introduction of typography, when the Venetians introduced morocco from the East and found out the virtues of calf. Books now became bound in oak boards covered with these leathers or in thick parchment or pig skin, old manuscripts often being cut up and of course destroyed for the purpose: boards, clasps, and bosses became obsolete, while silken embroidery maintained a precarious existence, dependent solely on the spasmodic efforts of accomplished amateurs whose tastes and inclinations were swayed by fashion. Finally, parchment disappeared and leather bindings held universal sway, and have so maintained it to our own time, though the English cloth-bound book is now employed whenever expense is an object.

Such is a short history of the development of the art of bookbinding, as necessary to be understood and remembered as any other branch of our subject.

Some of the better-known and more valuable descriptions of ornamental bindings, whether Italian, French, or English, derive their entire importance by reason of their having come from the libraries of noted collectors, who bound their books after a model pattern. Many of these specimens are of the greatest rarity and often of great value. As works of art, too, they are frequently far superior to anything that can be, or at any rate is, produced at the present day. A really well bound book by Le Gascon, or one of the Eves, for example, is a beautiful object. The covers, of the choicest calf or morocco, are tooled in patterns, *i.e.*, hand engraved, in gold; the edges are of gilt, *gauffré*, that is to say, designs are impressed on them also; the whole is a splendid specimen of bibliopegistic skill. Such artists as these disdained blind tooling, where the patterns are worked out and left without their meed of gold. Half-bound volumes with their back and corners of leather and their sides of vulgar paper or boards they were either ignorant of or despised.

All this excellence of course cost money, which then, as now, was in the hands of the few, and it must not for a moment be supposed that examples of high-class binding were at all common even during the era in which they were produced. They are scarcer now, for time and fire have claimed their share of spoil, but it was only the great collectors of almost unlimited means, popes, kings, and cardinals, and their favourites, who could afford at any time to furnish a library where beautiful bindings predominated.

These collections have for the most part been dispersed over the world, and an amateur of the true old-fashioned type will not allow himself to be looked upon as fortunate, if his shelves do not contain one or two examples at least from the magnificent libraries of brother amateurs long since passed away.

The Italians were the first to awake to the enormity of binding their books in pig skin, or encasing them between clumsy wooden boards; and readily profiting by the teachings of the great master painters, who made Italy their peculiar home, they began to use calf and morocco, elaborately tooled to geometrical patterns. Leo X. (1513-21) had a good library, and one book at least is extant, bound by an Italian artist in red morocco, with the Papal arms on the sides. Some years previously to this, Aldus Manutius had bound his own books at Venice, and he took as much care of their dress as he did of the text. Some of these bindings appear to be imitations of the designs sculptured on the walls of mosques, and it was from the East therefore that the great Venetian school obtained its first instruction in the art. The book lover rejoices exceedingly when he meets with any of these ancient Italian bindings, but if he can only possess a Maioli, his cup of happiness literally overflows.

This Maioli—who or what he was are alike unknown—this Maioli had an extensive library, and all his books were sumptuously bound in the choicest leathers and tooled in gold on the backs and sides. On an embossed shield was the title of the work, and underneath, that inscription afterwards imitated by Grolier, "Tho Maioli et Amicorum". Let not the collector be deceived however:—there were two Maiolis: Thomasso, above mentioned, whose choice bindings are sought after all the world over, and Michel, whose artistic tastes were less fully developed, and who perhaps knew better than to invite his friends to borrow from his store.

Cardinal Bonelli (1541-98) and Canevari, the physician to Pope Urban VIII. (1559-1625), were both enamoured of costly bindings, the latter especially, for on the sides of his books appears a gorgeous object representing Apollo in gold, driving his chariot in blue or red over a silver sea.

Lorenzo de Medici, Prince of Florence, scholar and patron of art and literature, called the Magnificent, who died in 1492, stamped his books with the Medici arms, together with a laurel branch and the motto *Semper*. Others of the Medici family had splendid libraries, and their books were often covered with silver and gold beautifully inlaid, after the designs of painters of the highest eminence.

Amongst other Italian collectors whose fondness for calf and morocco carried them perhaps just a little too near the border line of extravagance, were Pietro Accolti, Cardinal of Ancona (1445-1532), Antonio Alemanni, the poet (1500), and Pasqual Cicogna, Doge of Venice, who died in 1595. Specimens from the libraries of any of these, and others besides, are sometimes worth far more than their weight in gold.

The Italian bookbinders were the instructors of the French, who subsequently rivalled and finally eclipsed their masters. At first the French merely imitated, but towards the close of the reign of Francis I. (*cir.* 1540), they struck out fresh lines of their own.

Jean Grolier is the representative collector of the early French school, but he was, at the same time, the most famous judge of bindings that the world has yet seen. He was born at Lyons in 1479, and died in 1565, having spent nearly the whole of his life in the collection of books. His opinion of French binders appears to have been the reverse of complimentary, for he went to Italy to find a workman after his own heart, and one who could be relied upon to satisfy his fastidious taste. Many people think that Grolier was by trade a bookbinder, but this is a mistake—he was merely an enthusiastic amateur who allowed his passion for bindings to become his master. Some of his designs he prepared himself; others are undoubted imitations of those adopted by Maioli, whom he so greatly admired, that even his motto is reproduced, with of course the necessary variation, "Io Grolierii et Amicorum". This appears on the sides of most of his books, and there is consequently no difficulty in identifying them. Others bear an emblem, and in a scroll, "Æque difficulter," and others again the words of the Psalmist arranged so as to form a triangle, "Portio mea Domine sit in terra viventium".[12] Most of Grolier's books were printed by Aldus at Venice, and they are generally found lettered on the back, a practice which was not in vogue before his day. But however bound, and whatever device, maxim, or motto he employed, the name of Grolier invariably causes great excitement among amateurs. The value of any of his books is proverbial, and their scarcity equally so. A rare book may occasionally be snapped up for a hundredth part of its worth, not so a magnificent specimen of binding, which courts further inquiries on the part of the vendor, and, as we all know, "further inquiries" are usually fatal to the would-be snapper-up of unconsidered valuables.

Louis de Sainte-Maure was a contemporary of Grolier, and like him an enthusiastic book hunter. His bindings are said to be even rarer still. They too are tooled

---

[12] See Guigard, *Armorial du Bibliophile,* vol. i. p. 248.

with geometrical figures, and on the side, in the centre, is the inscription, "Invia virtuti nulla est via".

Diana of Poitiers, the mistress of Henri II. of France (*cir.* 1540), was another famous collector, who spent vast sums on binding her books. The designs were made in all probability by Le Petit Bernard, one of the most famous engravers of his day, and her books, like those of Grolier, were gold tooled on both back and sides. Diana's device consisted of a bow and a crescent, sometimes with a sheaf of arrows. Those books which the infatuated Henri sent to his mistress bear the H. surmounted by a crown and flanked by the *fleur-de-lys*. Henri was himself a collector of no mean order, and his volumes, like those belonging to the fair Diana, have their countless worshippers. The king, whatever the laxity of his morals, was a stickler for etiquette, and drew a wide distinction between a mistress and a wife. Some of his books are stamped with the interwoven initials H. and D., and ornamented with the usual emblems of the chase, but no crown is observable. That makes its appearance over a solitary H., banished, so to speak, to the remoter regions of the cover. Sometimes the initials are changed to H. C., interwoven and surmounted by the crown, and then we know that Henri chose to honour his wife Catherine de Medicis with notice.

Diana's library at the Château d'Anet was dispersed by auction in 1723: it contained volumes of the most varied descriptions, lives of the saints and lewd songs jostling one another with impudent familiarity.

Catherine de Medicis herself had the taste of Diana for beautiful bindings, and kept a staff of workmen, who vied with each other in the production of beautiful specimens of ornamentation. She had the mania of the true book collector, for on the death of the Maréchal de Strozzi, she laid violent hands on his choice and valuable library, promising to pay for it sometime, but ultimately dying herself without doing so.

The books of Francis I. (1515-47), if bound for his use while Dauphin of France, are marked with a dolphin, in addition to the ordinary kingly stamps of the Royal Arms, a salamander, and the letter F. The motto in each case is the same: "Nutrio et extinguo". Specimens of binding having the dolphin are extraordinarily rare.

Henri III. (1574-89) did much to reduce the extravagant cost of bookbinding, for, in 1583, he made a decree that ordinary citizens should not decorate any single book with more than four diamonds, or the nobility with more than five; he himself and a few other scapegraces of the Royal House were under no restriction. The same King instituted the order of the "Penitents" as some little compensation for a life of shameless vice and crime, and celebrated the occurrence by the invention of a new binding, the originality of which is undoubted. On black morocco, and sometimes with the Arms of France, appear a death's head, cross-bones, tears, and other emblems of woe, including a joke in the form of a motto, "Spes mea Deus". Henri, when Duke of Anjou, loved Mary of Clèves, and subsequently consoled himself for her untimely death by binding a quantity of books in his library. Skulls, tears, and *fleurs-de-lys* are thrown about in profusion; the motto, "Memento mori," looks out at you from among floreated ornaments; Jesus and Marie are placed on a level. When ordered to attend the Court after the death of his beloved Mary, he made his appearance in a black robe, embroidered all over with the usual funereal emblems.

The gloomy bindings of Henri III. brought on a reaction, giving rise to a style of decoration known as *à la fanfare*. No sooner was the King gathered to his fathers than his sister, Margaret of Valois, exchanged the death's heads for a fanciful decoration, consisting of a profusion of foliage, sprinkled with daisies. Bindings of this period are very choice, but not so elaborate as the development of the *fanfare* eventually made them. The foliage became much more delicate, and the clusters of leaves and flowers at last resembled lace work, under the magic touch of the great binder Le Gascon.

We now leave Royal personages, and descend to a lower level, meeting at the very threshold the historian Thuanus, better known as De Thou (1553-1617). This celebrated amateur and patron of bookbinding was an intimate friend of Grolier, and president of the Paris Parliament in the reign of Henri IV. All his books, of which he possessed a large number, were bound in morocco or gilded calf skin in a style which varied with the different periods of his life. His bachelor's library was embellished with his arms in silver, between two branches of laurel, with his name below. After his marriage in 1587, his wife's escutcheon is stamped alongside his own with the initials J. A. M. below, and also on the backs of his volumes. During his life as a widower, a wreath of twining-stems tipped with red berries, and his own and dead wife's initials interlaced, take the place of other ornaments. After his second marriage in 1603, his new wife's escutcheon appears in conjunction with his own, but the initials are changed to J. A. G.

This splendid library remained intact for more than 200 years, and it was not until 1677 that it was sold almost as it stood to the Marquis de Ménars. At his death in 1718, it was purchased by Cardinal de Rohan, but in 1789, his heirs, impoverished by legal proceedings, were compelled to disperse the collection. The binders principally employed by De Thou were the Eves (Nicholas, Clovis, and Robert), whose splendid workmanship is a model for such of our modern binders as follow the higher branches of the art.

Le Gascon, the binder to the Duke of Orleans, who seems to have flourished between the years 1620 and 1640, was another workman of the first rank. The Duke was a great collector, whose shelves were covered with green velvet, garnished with gold lace and fringe, and whose bindings by Le Gascon were similarly ornamented.

Among the large number of French bibliophiles who now appeared on the scene, and competed with each other in the beauty of their bindings, one or two must necessarily be mentioned, since the modern collector envies or admires their taste.

Chancellor Séguier, at the end of the seventeenth century, employed Ruette to make the bindings *au mouton d'or*, which graced his shelves; and a little later still, the Baron de Longepierre utilised the well-known ornament of the Golden Fleece, which, when found on any book, no matter how intrinsically worthless, greatly enhances its price. These are the prizes of book collecting, seldom met with, and always strongly competed for.

The Colberts stamped the sides of their books with their crest, in which the climbing adder is always conspicuous. There were no less than seven members of this family who loved books, and all embellished them with the adder in a shield surmounted by a crown.

Nicholas (1680) and Charles Louis Fouquet (1684-1761) each adopted the coat of arms with a squirrel—looking for all the world like a lion—and the motto, "Quo non ascendam". Cardinal Mazarin, who died at Vincennes on the 9th of March, 1661, had many devices, the most common of which is the coat of arms, consisting of an axe bound up in a bundle of fasces, and surmounted by a cardinal's hat. These and many other figures which generations of bibliophiles have caused to be tooled on their books, point conclusively to what library any given specimen formerly belonged, though, as might be expected, it is sometimes a matter of great difficulty, or even impossibility, to identify particular volumes. Some amateurs discarded their own crests, and adopted others, for reasons which are not apparent, while women, as, for example, the Duchesse du Maine, who decorated her books at Sceaux with a golden bee-hive, appear to have possessed the most intricate armorial bearings, or to have been guided by mere caprice, in their choice of emblems. Many books bearing crests or coats of arms cannot, therefore, be identified, and for this reason, amongst others, the few books which have been written on this branch of the art of binding are necessarily incomplete. One of the best—which, moreover, contains some hundreds of woodcuts illustrative of various devices—is Guigard's *Armorial du Bibliophile*, 2 vols., 8vo, Paris, 1870-3, but this is strictly confined to French devices. Even Hobson's choice, however, is often better than none.[13]

Although the sixteenth century was *par excellence* the era of ornamental bindings, it cannot be said that England made much progress in the art. Up to the reign of Elizabeth we seem to have persisted in the use of clumsy oak boards or stiff parchment covers, and when a really choice and expensive binding was required, it took the form of embroidered silks and velvets. Queen Elizabeth herself was very expert in this method of ornamentation, which continued to exist, in all probability, simply because it was fashionable.

The first English bookbinder of any repute was John Reynes, a printer, who lived in the reigns of Henry VII. and VIII. Specimens of his work are very rare, though, when compared with the French bindings of the same date, they appear miserably inferior. The truth is that England was—and, indeed, is—much behind some other countries in everything relating to bibliography, and binding in particular.

Robert Dudley, the great Earl of Leicester, was the first English book collector who was possessed of any degree of taste. His cognisance of the "bear and the ragged staff" appears on the sides of a (generally) quite plain binding, although sometimes a rough attempt at ornamentation is found. Archbishop Parker, and Burgh-

[13] Mr. Quaritch, the bookseller, has in preparation a *Dictionary of English Book Collectors*, somewhat after the scheme of M. Guigard's book.

ley the Lord Treasurer, had good libraries of well-bound books, and one specimen from Bothwell's collection is known to exist. This, the *Larismetique et Géometrie* of La Roche, *Lyon*, 1538, was in the possession of the late Mr. Gibson-Craig, and is mentioned by him in his *Fac-similes of Old Book-Binding*. It is in the original calf gilt, with gilt *gaufré* edges, and on the sides are the arms of James Hepburn, Earl of Bothwell. Although Bothwell is known to have possessed literary tastes, books from his library are excessively rare. This fine book belonged originally to the family of Forbes of Tolquhon, and a signature and date 1588 written on the title-page show that it had been acquired by them a few years after the outlawry and death of the original proprietor. At the Gibson-Craig sale this fine specimen was knocked down for £81.

James I. was a bibliophile, as well as a reputed *savant*, and paid much attention to the binding of his books, some of which, now to be seen in the British Museum, are ornamented with thistles and *fleurs-de-lys*. Lord Clarendon, who died in 1674, had a very fine collection of books, many of which were bound by Notts, the most experienced English workman of that day, and who was, it appears, also patronised by Pepys, the diarist.

It was not, however, until the eighteenth century that we made in this country any real advance in bookbinding. Robert Harley, the first Earl of Oxford (1661-1724), had established a library, and this had not only been added to by his son, but bound in a most expensive manner, by two workmen named Elliott and Chapman, who seem to have attained a certain amount of proficiency, and whose efforts gave rise to a new style of ornamentation known as the "Harleian". Though much inferior to the Continental designs, this had a beauty of its own, and was a vast improvement upon anything hitherto attempted by English binders.

Thomas Hollis, the *littérateur* and antiquary, who died in 1774, bound his extensive collection in calf, adding, in each instance, a device suitable to the contents of the work. Thus, as the owl is the symbol of wisdom, his scientific books bear the figure of an owl stamped on the covers. Military works have the short Roman stabbing sword, and so on.

If we except, perhaps, the French emigrants who made their home in this country at the end of the eighteenth century, there really was no binder of any note until the advent of Roger Payne (1739-1797). This workman, though dissolute, had, nevertheless, a reputation in his line second to none. In person, he is stated to have been dirty and untidy, but certainly neither of these defects appear in his bindings, which, though not, as a rule, heavily gilt, are tooled to neat classical or geometrical designs after the Venetian style. Where Payne made his mark was, perhaps, in the *appropriateness* of his bindings. His judgment, in this respect, appears to have been sound and popular.

After Payne followed Walther, Charles Hering, and Charles Lewis, all of whom, the last particularly, did very good work. In more recent times still we have Hayday, Rivière, Francis Bedford, Ramage, and last, but by no means least, Zaehnsdorf, whose son yet carries on business in London.

The ordinary cloth bindings, such as we see every day in the booksellers' shops, are purely English, and have been in use since 1823, when they were invented by Lawson, and adopted by Pickering, the publisher. In Continental countries they use paper covers, and even the most expensive works are issued originally in this form. There they bind their books after publication if they are found to be worth binding. In this country cloth is now largely used, and is certainly a great improvement on the old clumsy covers of a bygone age, or on the paper wrappers of this.

Bookbinding in the higher styles is now done fairly well in England, though, in the opinion of many, the workmanship is not equal to that of the French artists of three hundred years ago.

CHAPTER XI.

ONE of the most difficult branches of bibliography is that which treats of the books to choose and those to avoid, with reference mainly to their pecuniary value. Few collectors, who are not specialists, care very much for the utility of their libraries; in many cases, indeed, it is not a question of utility at all, but of extent, though I apprehend that no one would wish to crowd his shelves with rubbish merely for the sake of filling them. As an immense proportion of the books which have been published during the sixteenth, seventeenth, eighteenth, and nineteenth centuries clearly come under that category, the collector has much to avoid, and stands in need of considerable experience to enable him to make a selection.

Naudé, the apologist for "great men suspected of magic," whose patron, by the way, was Cardinal Mazarin, had a method of purchasing which, if not unique, was at any rate uncommon. His favourite plan was to buy up entire libraries, and sort them at his leisure; or when these were not available in the bulk, he would, as Rossi relates, enter a shop with a yard measure in his hand, and buy his books by the ell. Wherever he went, paper and print became scarce: "the stalls he encountered were like the towns through which Attila had swept with ruin in his train". Richard Heber, the bibliotaph, too, had collections of miscellaneous books at Paris, Antwerp, Brussels, and other continental towns, to say nothing of London, where the aristocracy among his treasures were deposited. The books were sold by auction after his death; the sale occupied 202 days, and flooded the market with rubbish—a worthy termination to a life of sweeping and gigantic purchases, made in the hope of acquiring single grains of wheat among his tons of worthless chaff.

But Naudé had the wealth of Mazarin at his back, and free licence to purchase as and where he would at the Cardinal's expense, while Heber was rich beyond the dreams of avarice; the modern book hunter, whose means we will suppose are limited, must discard the yard measure and the scales, and rely on his judgment, taking care to get the utmost value for his money. He will have to make up his mind to buy or not to buy on the spur of the moment, for while he is consulting his books of reference at home, a golden opportunity may be missed. This is his capital difficulty, and one which it will take years of experience to surmount, for there is no *vade mecum* capable of being carried in the waistcoat pocket, which will enable him to spot a rarity at a glance; nothing, in fact, which can compensate for a lack of practical knowledge. I have often thought that a register of scarce but mean-looking English books, of such a convenient size as to be carried in the palm of the hand, might be of assistance to those who haunt the stalls, and delve among the rubbish usually to be found there; some day, perhaps, it may be worth while to try the experiment, *sed Gloria, quantalibet quid erit; si gloria tantum est*? What will be the value of ever so much glory, if it be glory and nothing else?

In turning over the contents of an old book-stall, the major portion of the heap will be found to consist of volumes of sermons, and other theological treatises, recipe books, odd historical volumes, and poetical effusions, besides periodical literature of the *Spectator* and *Tatler* brand. Books of this class are, as a rule, merely rubbish; but still there are a few exceptions. Sermons of John Knox and Dr. Sacheverell, or any of Mather's tracts, are invariably worth purchasing; as also are first editions of sermons by Cardinals Manning or Newman. Early editions of Mrs. Glasse's cookery book, or any recipe books of the seventeenth century, may safely be speculated in; so may early editions of poetical works, if written by authors whose reputation subsequently became established. Third, fourth, or later editions are seldom of much value, no matter who the author may be, and no matter of what character or description, provided they come under one or other of the heads enumerated above. In purchasing books of the class generally found on second-hand stalls, there are two preliminary questions to be asked: first, was the author of sufficient reputation to make his name well known? and secondly, is the particular copy of his works offered for sale an early edition? If an affirmative answer can be given to each of these inquiries, it will be advisable to tender the small sum likely to be asked, and to run the risk.

Another point to be observed is that where a printer's device appears on the title-page, or indeed on any other part of an *old* book, it is more likely than not to have a value, and it ought never to be passed over without a careful scrutiny.

Should the collector be fortunate enough to pick up a rare French book, his best policy will be to have it suitably bound in France by a first-rate binder. Though already valuable, its importance will be still further increased by this manœuvre; for when the inevitable day of parting shall arrive, the French bibliophiles will be more inclined to welcome native talent than any English imitation of it.

Volumes containing separate tracts should always be examined, as it sometimes happens that rare pieces are found bound up with a mass of worthless matter. I once heard of original editions of two of Molière's plays being found in this way; and as these stand pretty much in the same position, so far as rarity and consequent value is concerned, to the early Shakespearean quartos, the importance of the "find" to the lucky discoverer can hardly be exaggerated. This is only another example of the rule which can never be too often repeated, since it can never be sufficiently understood. If the author is "big enough," and the edition is early enough, buy. The probability is you may not realise the full importance of what you have got until you have had time to consult some book of reference; it may indeed turn out that a wretched and dirty reprint has done duty for the original, or it may so be that the book is worthless on its merits. This is one of the risks of book collecting, and, it may be added, one of its charms. Hundreds of thousands of dead and forgotten books must be annually disposed of, for nominal sums, in London alone, and there is no telling how often these and others may have been turned over and flung aside by passers-by before they eventually find a market. Among all this profusion of rubbish, a certain percentage of valuable pieces must necessarily exist, and these, from the very circumstances under which they are offered for sale, will be unknown, and more or less unbound and uncut. Every year some of these princes in disguise are rescued from the wind and rain, and henceforth considered a fair exchange for gold instead of copper; but alas! we cannot both eat our cake and have it too. "Finds," as they are called, are not so numerous as they once were, nor hucksters so ignorant as in the merry days of Dibdin and Burton, to say nothing of such foreign Nimrods as Colbert, Grolier, and the great Pixérécourt.

The same rules which guide the haunter of the stalls are suitable to those who purchase from the regular booksellers. There is so much to be learned, so many artificial rules and distinctions to be observed in everything relating to books, that mistakes are of frequent occurrence. Ignorant assistants have before now unwittingly thrown shabby little books, like Burns' Poems (Kilmarnock, 1786), into the sixpenny-box at the shop door; others have been too lazy to sort the "parcels" as they have come in from the auctioneers, and have bundled the whole contents into the same repository. There are a hundred and one accidents in favour of the book hunter, but he needs experience in order to take advantage of them, and this cannot be got without the expenditure of much time and money and the suffering of many disappointments, which, indeed, seem to increase as he grows older, rather than to diminish. This is doubtless because the sphere of his operations becomes wider until it exceeds that of his experience; the seventh age of the Bibliophile is even as his first.

Apart from the books which are fashionable for the time being and invariably command fancy prices, there are others which may be styled "standards," that is to say, are sold over and over again, both by auction and private contract, for sums which vary only according to condition. These for the most part are in several volumes, 8vo, frequently also in 4to or folio. Their very appearance precludes any prospect of a bargain; indeed the purchaser, unless well versed in book-lore, stands a very good chance of paying for mere bulk. When the library at Sion College took fire, the attendants at the risk of their lives rescued a pile of books from the flames, and it is said that the librarian wept when he found that the porters had taken it for granted that the value of a book was in exact proportion to its size. To this day the impression that big books contain wisdom is all but universal. This has always been so, as witness the temporary reputation of Nicholas de Lyra, who wrote and printed 1800 folios of Commentary on the Bible, and of Aldrovandus, whose thirteen large folio volumes on General Zoology (1599-1668) have greatly perplexed the scientific world ever since they were published. Let not the collector be led away by massive tomes, nor imagine that standard works of acknowledged reputation can often be got for less than they are worth.

Of late years there has been a violent competition for books and even tracts published in or in any way relating to the American Continent provided only that they were published during the sixteenth, seventeenth, and sometimes also the eighteenth centuries. Thus Cotton's *Abstract of the Laws of New England*, 1641; *The Description of Jamaica*, 1657; Brereton's *Relation of the Discoverie of the North Part of Virginia*, 1602, and many other obscure little 4to tracts—not books—would be cheap at twenty guineas each, while others are worth even more. American collectors are largely responsible for this. In the same way treatises of any kind which have a Scotch local interest, and are dated about the same period, are always worth two or three guineas at the least, and in many cases far more than those amounts.

The earliest book printed in Scotland is *The Knightly Tale of Golagrus and Gawane and other ancient poems* (Edinburgh, 1508), 4to, which was reprinted in fac-simile under the superintendence of Dr. Laing in 1827. As might be expected, the original is so scarce as to be unprocurable, and even the reprint is of considerable value. Early Scotch-printed books by such workmen as Walter Chepman, Androu Myllar, Andro Hart, Alexander Arbuthnot, Thomas Davidson, Anthony Marlar, James Watson, Andrew Anderson and his widow the would-be monopolist, Robert Freebairn, and several others, some of whom carried on business into the eighteenth century, should never be overlooked or discarded. These are just the kind of books which are occasionally discovered on stalls in obscure streets, and which may be expected to be bought for a few pence. They are scarce, of course, or it would not be worth while to mention them; but they look insignificant, and many, for anything I know, may this very day be making their weary pilgrimage on costermongers' barrows in the New Cut, despised and rejected of men.

Specimens of typography from the presses of Caxton, Wynkyn de Worde, and other early English printers, some of which have already been mentioned, are essentially curiosities, and it is almost useless to hope for even the semblance of a bargain so far as they are concerned. Still, occasional finds are from time to time reported from out-of-the-way villages whose inhabitants have not yet wakened from their mediæval slumbers, and great is the rejoicing of the explorer, and many the paragraphs with which the discovery is heralded in the newspapers. The collector who is fortunate enough to come across a work of this class—he can hardly expect a repetition of such extraordinary luck—will have crowned his labours, be they great or small, and can henceforth pride himself on his success. If he never handles a book again, he will have earned his laurels.

Inferior County Histories in one volume, generally 8vo, are always worth buying if they can be got for a few pence, as is often the case, for there are very few of them which are not worth as many shillings at the least. Topographical works are now being inquired for to a much greater extent than was the case several years ago, and the booksellers can dispose of almost any quantity. Such examples as are likely to be casually met with are, however, very small game; yet they represent the average amount of success likely to be achieved at one time in these days of widespread knowledge. The demand for book rarities is very great, and every hole and corner, likely and unlikely, is periodically ransacked by booksellers' "jackals," to say nothing of the army of amateurs ever on the look-out for bargains. Accident is, however, productive of occasional successes, and every man has, or may have, if he thinks proper to put it to the test, an equal chance.

In addition to the ready-made bargains, which do more than anything else to delight the heart of the book lover and encourage him to further exertions, there is such a thing as playing upon popular likes and dislikes, or, in other words, speculating on the vagaries of fashion. At present the rage is for original editions of modern authors, principally those with plates, coloured or uncoloured. Some day the fashion will change, and books hitherto neglected will suddenly take their place and increase many times in value. Such books should be bought while they are cheap, and they doubtless would be if there was such a thing as a literary barometer capable of forecasting the state of the market; but there is not, and it is impossible to foretell the direction in which the mass of book lovers will turn when once they are tired of picture-books.

Every bookseller is of necessity a speculator, for it is his business to buy at a low price and to sell at a higher. The amateur, however, should, if he would preserve his title, abstain from traffic of this kind and be satisfied to pay for the privilege of forming a library without regard to the ultimate profit or loss. His pleasure should consist in acquisition and the opportunity afforded of fondling his store while there is time, for he may be absolutely certain that the whole assortment—book-cases, shelves, and all—will find their way to the auctioneer directly he has done with them. This mournful prospect has been the indirect means of founding a new school, that of the semi-amateurs, which, while claiming for itself all the attributes of the book lover, has, nevertheless, an eye to the main chance, and is prepared at a moment's notice to transfer an entire collection *inter vivos* if the required sum be forthcoming. As an ardent Waltonian would regard a brother of the angle who went a-fishing with the object of selling his catch, so the old-fashioned bibliophile views this degenerate school—that is to say, with unfeigned disgust. It makes no difference, nay, if anything it is an aggravation, that the culprit is "well up" in his subject and knows a book when he sees one. "Fancy!" says a member of the old academy, "here is an educated man who for years has occupied his leisure hours in studies the most delightful, and among friends the most courteous and refined. He knows them, can put his hand upon any in the dark, and yet— —;" but here the power of words fails to describe the heartless greed which alone could send a row of life's companions to the block. Nevertheless this is being done every day, and, however vexed the respectable book lover may be, the fact remains that the new school is just now showing remarkable activity and is running the booksellers very close indeed. The advisability of purchasing depends upon the answer to a single question, "Will this book go up?" Never mind the author, or a syllable of what he wrote, but take especial care to see that the work is perfect, clean, and uncut, and then ask yourself this solitary question. This is the first and last commandment of the semi-amateur, whose method of procedure it may be interesting to analyse.

Let us suppose that a London publisher advertises a new edition of some famous work, tastefully got up and luxuriously bound and illustrated. The issue of course is limited, as the price is high, and discriminating purchasers must be tempted. The old-fashioned amateur is not to be charmed because he persuades himself that there is plenty of time, and what matter if a few years later he has to pay a slightly enhanced price? The book will be worth it, for it will be scarce, and, moreover, have attained a respectable degree of antiquity, and so he passes it by. Not so the new school, which we will assume has answered its solitary question in the affirmative. The edition is snapped up in a moment, and single members will buy as many duplicates as they can afford to invest in—buy to sell again ultimately, and in the meantime to gloat over, like so many jackdaws eying a secreted heap of stolen goods. This is commonly called "cornering" an edition; and when several persons possessing the same opinions and the same tastes join their forces, it will readily be perceived that if a book will not go up of its own accord it may readily be forced up by judicious retention and self-denial. This, of course, is nothing more nor less than Stock-Exchange speculation, and it is satisfactory to find that sometimes the greedy purchaser makes a mistake and is saddled with a small stock of waste-paper.

As previously stated in the fifth chapter, a book which has perhaps been cornered as often as any other, and never successfully, is Ottley's *Italian School of Design*, on large paper, with proof impressions. The published price was £25 4s., the present value is about £3 by auction. Here is a dreadful falling off, and the adherents of the new school have never yet been able to understand the reason, or to cease persuading themselves that the day must surely come when the book will go up. If anything, however, it is going down, and in the opinion of many experts it can never again take a respectable position in the market.

Another book which has also been speculated in, and with even more disastrous results still, is *Hogarth's Works*, from the original plates, restored by Heath, and published by Baldwin and Cradock, in 1822, at £50. This is a large and sumptuous work, with a secret pocket at the end, in which are, or should be, found the three suppressed plates. The present auction value is not much more than £4, and, judging from appearances, it is very unlikely to get any higher. How many people have burned their fingers over these two tempting works it would be very difficult even to guess; suffice it to say, that the amateur speculator often has half-a-dozen of each on his shelves, and in nine cases out of ten he finds them an encumbrance and a loss. As John Hill Burton truly says, "No good comes of gentlemen amateurs buying and selling". This is, of course, as it should be; but rejoicing at the fate of the enemy is likely to be turned into gall when it is discovered that defeat is bolstered up with the inevitable axiom "Better luck next time".

It cannot be denied that, from a practical everyday stand-point, the collector who buys to sell has everything in his favour. Why should he not employ his knowledge to advantage? why be compelled to stock his library at a loss which will fall chiefly on his immediate descendants? why suffer the pain and mortification of ever remembering that after all his books are only lent to him on hire, and that as others have parted with the identical volumes before, so he must also part with them in his turn? The pleasure of possession is mixed with an alloy which is disquieting to the man who loves his books too well. Still, after all, there is one pleasure which the votaries of the new school can never hope to enjoy, and that is the communion with old friends. Their books are strangers, and even though they should learn them by heart, they would be strangers still. The remembrance of happy hours spent with a lost volume is to them as nothing compared with the ringing metal which replaces it; or to put the case as pleasantly as possible, we will say that the speculator regards a book as possessing an interest quite apart from its literary or domestic value. How such an one would hunger after the treasures secured by an eager collector at a fishmonger's shop in Hungerford Market some fifty years ago—"Autograph signatures of Godolphin, Sunderland, Ashley, Lauderdale, Ministers of James II., accounts of the Exchequer Office signed by Henry VII. and Henry VIII., wardrobe accounts of Queen Anne, secret service accounts marked with the 'E. G.' of Nell Gwynne, a treatise on the Eucharist in the boyish hand of Edward VI., and a disquisition on the Order of the Garter, in the scholarly writing of Elizabeth," all of which, as Mr. Rogers Rees narrates, had been included in waste-paper cleared out of Somerset House at £7 a ton.

Lector House believes that a society develops through a two-fold approach of continuous learning and adaptation, which is derived from the study of classic literary works spread across the historic timeline of literature records. Therefore, we aim at reviving, repairing and redeveloping all those inaccessible or damaged but historically as well as culturally important literature across subjects so that the future generations may have an opportunity to study and learn from past works to embark upon a journey of creating a better future.

This book is a result of an effort made by Lector House towards making a contribution to the preservation and repair of original ancient works which might hold historical significance to the approach of continuous learning across subjects.

HAPPY READING & LEARNING!

LECTOR HOUSE LLP
E-MAIL: lectorpublishing@gmail.com

...ntent.com/pod-product-compliance
... LLC

...26
...B/1062